THE PROFESSIONAL'S GUIDE TO

FINANCIAL
SERVICES
MARKETING

THE PROFESSIONAL'S GUIDE TO

FINANCIAL SERVICES MARKETING

BITE-SIZED INSIGHTS FOR CREATING EFFECTIVE APPROACHES

JAY NAGDEMAN

WILEY

John Wiley & Sons, Inc.

Library of Congress Cataloging-in-Publication Data:
Nagdeman, Jay, 1939–
    The professional's guide to financial services marketing : bite-sized insights for creating effective approaches / Jay Nagdeman.
        p.   cm.
    Includes bibliographical references and index.
    ISBN 978-0-470-41079-0 (cloth)
1. Financial services industry–Marketing.   I. Title.
    HG173.N24 2009
    332.1068'8–dc22   2008045573

Contents

"What businesses are we in?" How management answers this question can have a significant impact on the company's ultimate success.

Every now and then a major marketing idea comes along that revolutionizes the way that marketers approach their craft. The most influential have a significant impact that lasts for decades.

Success, in the form of rapid growth and high margins, comes most often to those organizations that understand the value of innovation and look beyond current competitive practices.

A knowledge and understanding of common product launch pitfalls can help marketers prevent financial product and service failures.

Financial services organizations are increasingly dependent on creative marketing ideas to achieve visibility and competitive differentiation in a cluttered marketplace.

It's not difficult to be a marketing hero when offerings are well received in the marketplace. The real challenge for most marketers is to find a way to "save the day" when there is a difficult sales situation.

21 **Unite and Conquer: Strength in Collaboration** 87

Since traditional organizational structures often lack
the resources to support expanded business models,
companies must devise creative new solutions.

22 **A Tale of Two Categories** 91

The Pareto Principle stands as a continual reminder to
focus 80 percent of your efforts on the 20 percent of
issues that will achieve 80 percent of your results.

23 **How Do You Measure Up?** 95

Effective marketing measurement—like marketing
itself—is an ongoing process that is both an art and a
science. This area is in its formative stages, but promises
to be a significant future trend.

IV **Promotion** 99

24 **The Secret of Successful Advertising** 101

While most advertising messages get lost in the clutter
and fail to accomplish their objectives, astute marketers
know the secrets to creating advertising that attracts
attention and gets results.

25 **Us vs. Them** 105

In the proper situation, targeted comparative
advertising can provide a powerful centerpiece
for a financial services organization's marketing
campaign.

26 **Speak Up** 109

Creatively conceived and effectively executed,
campaigns utilizing a corporate spokesperson can take
an organization one step further in its quest to
effectively deliver its marketing messages.

Preface

The financial services industry always seems to be living at the end of one era and the start of the next. Rapid change continually obsoletes yesterday's strategies and tactics and creates the need for new approaches that directly address current challenges. This constant evolution presents new problems for financial services organizations and new opportunities for marketers. In recent years the pace of these transitions has accelerated significantly.

The financial services industry began another new era in 2008. Transformational events reshaped the industry and created a new reality. Never has there been a greater need for the influence of marketing to help a firm carve out its future. If there has ever been a time for companies to make innovative marketing an important part of their business mix, that time is now. This appears, therefore, to be a good time to share the lessons I have learned over a career of watching marketing eras come and go.

I thank the many clients who have shared their trust and marketing concerns with our firm over the years. They may not realize how significantly they have contributed to this book. They have taught me much and many have become friends as well as clients. They have allowed me to gain a very broad perspective on marketing issues and the difference that financial services marketing can make to the success of corporate strategies and tactics. I am grateful for the experiences that we have had together.

My colleagues at Suasion Resources, especially my long-time assistant, Trudie McConnell, have been continually supportive. I owe special thanks to Carol Cole, who thoroughly reviewed the manuscript. After almost two decades of working with me, she understands my thinking and has an excellent grasp of financial services marketing. I am appreciative for her invaluable comments and suggestions.

I have been blessed and inspired by the unwavering support that I receive from those who are near and dear. I dedicate this book to the women in my life, who are, in order of appearance, Lorraine, Meredith, Sydney and Laurel.

Today financial services marketers have to battle much more than the competition. They must also overcome the clutter that increasingly pervades the marketplace. Ironically, far too many firms seem to think that the way to succeed in a marketplace overflowing with too many products and services, features and benefits is to respond with more of the same. To succeed in this highly competitive environment, financial organizations must instead innovate and develop approaches that will enable them to stand out in the marketplace as well as outshine the competition.

Each new era wrestles with old questions in new ways. My goal is to provide the foundation for some new answers by providing a personal perspective on many different aspects of the marketing discipline and discussing how they apply to financial services. I hope these observations will spark ideas that will help you develop new approaches that will successfully address the challenges of the eras ahead.

Foreword

The More Things Change, the More They Stay the Same

Ken Dolan, Chairman
The Dolan Group of Companies

It seems like a hundred years ago since I passed the New York Stock Exchange "Series 7" exam that allowed me to do securities transactions with public investors. The year was 1971. Since that time, I never really left the financial service business, serving first as a financial sales professional (career #1) and then, with my wife, Daria, as a member of the national media (career #2) for more than twenty years.

Many things have changed in the financial services marketing industry since 1971. In many ways, however, the challenges for financial services marketing professionals today are, in broad concept, very much the same as those I faced as a rookie broker. My charge was to engage potential investors who may be interested in a wide range of financial products and services *and* convert them to profitable clients for my firm.

But, not so fast! Today's typical financial services prospects are more educated than they were almost forty years ago and when it comes to financial information, they expect to get only what they want, when they want it and how (in what form) they want to receive it!

How then do you effectively distinguish your firm's marketing message and brand in this contemporary marketplace environment?

Marketing dollars can be a powerful force in the hands of a financial services marketing professional who is focused on the long term and willing to try new and differentiated approaches. In my opinion, the need for financial services marketing professionals who think out-of-the-box has never been more pronounced than it is *right now*!

Enter *The Professional's Guide to Financial Services Marketing*, written by Jay Nagdeman, a nationally respected financial services marketing consultant who has been Daria's and my friend for almost thirty years. Over the years, I have seen his firm, Suasion Resources, take on some daunting challenges and repeatedly apply a systematic mix of marketing approaches to lead clients to growth and prosperity. This book draws on the experience of this Master Marketer. It is designed to provoke thought and innovative marketing thinking for anyone in the financial services business—not just corporate types—who want to, and *must*, work smarter rather than harder. It provides challenges, insights and encouragement for financial services professionals who are not committed to business as usual and are willing to discard convention.

Are *you* up to the challenge? Well, it depends.

- Are you looking for another *how-to* book on the financial services business in general, and financial services marketing in particular, written by the latest *hot* guru? *The Professional's Guide to Financial Services Marketing* is not for you. Don't waste your money.
- Are you looking for a helpful and actionable guide, that is (1) designed to provoke innovative thought that can help you, the financial services professional, in your quest to create marketing innovation that will help your firm increase revenues and profitability in an increasingly competitive and fragmented

information environment *and* (2) written by a financial services marketing professional who has helped companies of all sizes prosper during both good and bad cycles over the past thirty years? *The Professional's Guide to Financial Services Marketing* is the book for you. You won't be able to put it down. You will never regret this investment!

Financial services firms face unique and often daunting marketing challenges. If you are involved in the industry in any way, you know exactly what I mean. You are selling products that no one can touch, taste or actually use. You have to comply with a host of ever-changing regulations that govern what you can say, how you can say it and, in some cases, even who you can say it to. At the same time, the competitive landscape is expanding and evolving. Sometimes it seems that everyone—from the big-box stores to web portals—is selling financial products and services. As a result, it is becoming harder and harder for financial services firms to even reach their potential customers, let alone distinguish their offerings in the marketplace. What then can you, as a financial services marketing professional, do to hone and improve your marketing programs? Many answers to this question can be found in *The Professional's Guide to Financial Services Marketing.*

Owning this book provides you with 24/7 access to some of the industry's most successful and innovative marketing thinking. It can provide you with insights and inspiration. It contains illustrations and vignettes taken from real-life marketing successes and failures. It also provides ideas that could help you turn successful consumer product marketing techniques into customized financial product marketing approaches. It can serve as a mentor, a resource, a reference tool or simply a compelling look at some often overlooked and misunderstood marketing approaches.

Whether you are an independent representative or agent, or the Marketing Director or CEO of a major financial services firm, *The Professional's Guide to Financial Services Marketing* provides thoughts, ideas and approaches that can help you become a more productive marketer.

—Ken Dolan

Ken and Daria Dolan have hosted more than 5,000 national radio and television shows on CNN, CNN.fn, CNBC, and on the WOR Radio Network across North America and Hawaii. They have also published five books on personal finance, appeared as guests on dozens of television shows such as *Wall Street Week,* and spoken to investors around the world. Through their media presence over the years, including on www.dolans.com and on their current weekly nationally syndicated radio show heard across North America and Hawaii, the Dolans have spoken to millions of Americans. Interacting personally with more than 60,000 callers to date on television and radio over dozens of personal finance topics, they represent a sort of a continuing market survey of America's perceived needs and desires in the area of financial services.

Introduction

Historically, the financial services industry has considered marketing a luxury, rather than a critical part of the business mix. With few exceptions, marketing budgets in the financial arena have been at or near the bottom of the corporate food chain and among the earliest victims when corporate profits are threatened. As a result, financial organizations have forfeited billions of dollars by failing to respect, learn and apply sophisticated marketing techniques.

Over the last few difficult decades the financial services industry has experienced significant structural changes. At the same time, however, financial services marketing remains primarily what it has always been: conservative, seriously underperforming and focused on some very expensive approaches. While financial services marketers increasingly use contemporary marketing terminology such as brand equity, share-of-wallet and lifetime customer value, most of their organizations still routinely employ traditional and quite often ineffective marketing approaches.

An essential prerequisite for marketing success in today's highly competitive financial services arena is sensitivity to the rapidly changing industry. The competitive landscape is undergoing a dramatic transformation fueled by

- rapidly evolving economic and market conditions
- the development of new products, services and distribution channels

- growing competition
- increased target market awareness made possible by information technology.

The marketplace has also become more segmented than ever before. As a result, successful financial services marketing must now understand and appeal to the psychoeconomic and demographic elements of discrete segments.

To achieve marketing success in this new environment, financial services firms—regardless of their size or industry segment—must discard convention and seek out the most effective ways to increase productivity and penetrate their target markets. Changing times require new concepts and new approaches. The marketer's challenge was effectively stated by Alvin Toffler:

> *The illiterate of the 21 century will not be those who cannot read or write, but those who cannot learn, unlearn and relearn.*

Filling the Financial Services Marketing Gap

Marketing is a topic about which much has been written, and presumably read, over the last several years. However, precious little of that marketing literature has addressed financial services marketing in a nonacademic vein. Financial marketers face challenges that do not exist in other sectors. They must adhere to strict regulatory guidelines and, most importantly, they must continually bear in mind that, above all else, they are not selling a company, a product or a service. They are selling TRUST.

Marketing is both an art and a science. It is an ever-evolving discipline that embraces a wide variety of concepts, guidelines, approaches and ideas. An effective financial marketing campaign results from the proper execution and balance of a variety of disparate elements. Successful marketers are those who continually explore the wealth of marketing variables—together with their possible combinations and permutations—to develop applications and innovations that can make a meaningful contribution to corporate success.

The Professional's Guide to Financial Services Marketing discusses a broad spectrum of financial services marketing topics in bite-sized pieces. It offers a different perspective on some basic marketing approaches and explores useful marketing concepts that are often overlooked by financial services practitioners. It also offers examples of how the application of various approaches and concepts can help the financial services sector to improve marketing reach and effectiveness.

Lessons from the Grocery Aisle

Consumer product marketing provides a wealth of examples of successful marketing. With a marketing mindset that is in direct contrast to the prevailing wisdom in the financial services sector, these companies have understood the need to fight for every inch of shelf space. Over the years, the consumer sector has not only refined basic marketing practices, it has also developed a wide range of techniques to improve marketing reach and performance. It has even been known to increase marketing and communications budgets during difficult times.

As a result, financial services professionals of all types can learn some very valuable and powerful lessons from their counterparts who are selling soap powder and soda pop. Therefore, this book offers extensive examples of successful marketing practices from the consumer products sector while always remaining mindful of the important distinctions between the two sectors.

Take It Personally

The purpose of this book is not to provide a "how-to" manual, but rather to offer practical information, examples and tips that will serve as thought provokers and provide financial services marketers with the ideas and insights that will enable them to improve their own marketing approaches and achieve ambitious marketing goals.

In processing this information, however, it is very important to understand that the difference between *adopt* and *adapt* is more than just semantics.

Revisiting the basics or studying past marketing successes—within or outside the financial services industry—is an excellent starting point. However, to become innovative, you must apply your own knowledge, experience and creativity to shrink-wrap those adapted marketing applications to your own situation. The result will be more effective marketing that will enable your firm to create greater competitive advantage.

The first footprint in the snow is distinctive—thereafter it often turns to mud! Success is the reward for those who establish their own marketing leadership position.

This book will be most useful for financial services professionals who know that it would be costly and unproductive to become "me too" marketers and follow the example of the large, deep-pocketed financial firms that spend lavishly on materials, advertising and promotion. These professionals emulate neither ostriches with their heads in the sand nor academicians with their heads in the clouds. They believe that pragmatic and innovative marketing can provide outstanding results.

What's in It for You

The Professional's Guide to Financial Services Marketing is directed to financial professionals looking for better ways to create the relevant marketplace differentiation and competitive advantage that will enable them to acquire and retain satisfied customers and increase productivity and profitability. The book is equally applicable to a small representative office and to executives of large financial services companies. Its focus on the financial sector enables the reader to gain a better understanding of both the breadth of marketing issues that financial services marketers face and the nuances that can have an enormous impact on the success of financial marketing campaigns.

However, this book is not just for those who wear a marketing title. It's written for those who are involved with financial services marketing in any way and willing to reflect on how sharpening different aspects of that marketing can help their organizations.

This book provides a 360-degree perspective on a variety of issues that, although often labeled as "marketing issues," can have great impact on an organization's productivity and profitability and make a significant difference to corporate success.

To succeed in today's more competitive marketplace, organizations must adopt a marketing point of view throughout the organization— not just in the marketing department. It is hoped, therefore, that this book will help all financial services practitioners to gain a better understanding of

- how to refine various approaches so that they will have greater marketplace appeal
- different innovative techniques that can create greater marketing success
- what parameters financial service marketing can comfortably occupy
- how different aspects of marketing can make a greater contribution to corporate success.

Whatever your segment of the financial service industry and whatever the size of your firm, this book offers strategic and tactical insights that can help you cost-effectively achieve better marketing results and greater profitability. After all, when you're doing it right, good marketing doesn't cost. It pays!

THE PROFESSIONAL'S GUIDE TO

FINANCIAL SERVICES MARKETING

I

CREATING AN EXTRAORDINARILY EFFECTIVE MARKETING ORGANIZATION

1
Getting Started

Welcome to *The Professional's Guide to Financial Services Marketing*. To get started, let's take a brief look at the current state of marketing affairs in the financial services industry.

Sales vs. Marketing

Many in the industry use the terms "marketing" and "sales" interchangeably. In fact, in many financial services firms the sales function is commonly referred to as "marketing." For example, independent organizations that provide an outsourced sales force for investment management firms are known as third-party marketers and their trade organization is called 3PM (The Third Party Marketing Association).

Peter Drucker, however, was able to draw a line between sales and marketing: "Marketing takes the ball and runs the first fifty yards, then hands off to sales, which runs for the touchdown." I can only add that marketing is also responsible for post-sales programs that ensure that the hard-won yardage is not subsequently lost. Since marketing is integral to almost every activity that takes place both before and after the sale is made, it is understandable that many confuse the two disciplines.

Strategic vs. Tactical Initiatives

The distinction between marketing strategy and marketing tactics is an important one that can be summarized as follows:

Marketing strategy determines what to say. Marketing tactics determine how and where to say it.

Experience shows that effective marketing requires strategic thinking more than it requires a big budget. Cost-effective marketing initiatives begin with a carefully crafted strategic approach that focuses resources where they will achieve the greatest returns.

Unfortunately, many financial services executives fail to distinguish between strategically-oriented, integrated marketing programs and specialized marketing implementation activities. For many, the "M-word" is clearly a synonym for advertising or various other forms of promotion and tactical implementation—from direct mail programs and brochures to convention activities and chachkas.

Successful marketers know that true marketing is not a single activity, but rather a disciplined, multifaceted process that employs a variety of integrated activities and approaches (e.g., strategy development, research, branding, segmentation, tactical implementation and communications programs). These marketers help their organizations develop integrated initiatives that express strategic intent and position their companies and products to build competitive advantage in carefully defined niche markets.

Marketing + Innovation

It is important to realize that marketing that is commonplace can lead to a dangerous place. Me-too marketing approaches all too often result only in frustration and squandered resources. Strategic marketing seeks to create relevant differentiation and competitive advantage with innovative approaches—either the innovative use of existing techniques or the creation and implementation of an entirely new approach. Most marketing professionals understand that the really successful marketing initiatives are those that break the mold and connect with the marketplace. Although the creation of innovative marketing approaches is an objective in most organizations, there is too often a sizeable gap between the aspirations to innovate and the execution of truly innovative concepts.

Reality vs. Perception

Marketing works in two realms: reality and perception. Marketing, by definition, seeks to maximize those elements that create favorable marketplace perceptions and minimize, if not ignore, those that don't. In fact, tactical marketing is generally just another name for perception management.

At the same time, however, it is essential that the disparity between perception and reality is not too great. *Success follows truth.* A company will enjoy long-term success only if it can deliver—or hopefully over-deliver—what it promises to the marketplace.

2

A Marketing Pop Quiz

Is your organization an extraordinarily effective marketing organization?

Before you answer that question, let's explore what it takes to be an extraordinarily effective marketing organization. We believe that marketing includes all those activities that impact how an organization is perceived by its various constituencies.

The Architecture of Perception

To effectively control marketplace perceptions, a company's decision makers must first see the organization as customers and prospects see it: from the outside in. Management, with its insider perspective, often overlooks the fact that every organization has its own *marketing DNA*, the sum of the myriad elements that impact market perceptions and help define and shape its marketplace persona. The important factors that contribute to marketing DNA go beyond generally accepted marketing tools such as the symbols, signage, stationery and business cards that form the organization's marketing signature or the look and content of its collateral materials.

An organization's marketing DNA is the sum of everything that communicates what the company stands for and helps all their

7

constituencies form their perceptions of the organization and its product/ service offerings. To illustrate, one contributor to marketing perceptions is an organization's *body language*, the composite of a wide variety of elements, including office space (e.g., location, condition, furniture and décor) and personnel (e.g., dress code, attitude and behavior). Every organization must ask itself if the messages these elements deliver to visitors, clients and employees are consistent with their written and verbal communications. This piece of perception architecture helps determine whether a company is sending the right signals or strongly contradicting the perceptions it wishes to create in the marketplace.

Marketing Redefined

Given the extent of an organization's perception architecture, we believe that a fair evaluation of marketing effectiveness should include an examination of not only the marketing department's efforts, but also the activities of every functional area that interfaces with clients, prospects or distribution channels. The fact is that many successful Japanese companies don't even have a Marketing Department. They believe that marketing should not be confined to a single department, but should rather be the duty of everyone who is engaged in helping the organization to achieve its goals for productivity, client acquisition and retention.

The conversion of a financial services organization into an effective marketing organization will assuredly strengthen corporate performance but, in most cases, will require organizational paradigm shifts. Companies can spend millions on branding campaigns and yet forget that their switchboard operator often creates the ever-important first impression. The challenge is two-fold: First, ensure that every individual, regardless of their position, realizes that many of their daily interactions are marketing acts that can help or hinder corporate success; and second, equip them to assume psychological ownership of their marketing support role.

Mobilizing an Effective Marketing Organization

The following are key issues that can impact an organization's marketing success:

- *Compensation*. Studies show that the best way to engender positive marketing behavior is to set clear, reasonable goals and then measure and reward bottom-line results. In addition, customer and teammate evaluations, rather than the boss's subjective judgment, can help focus the entire team on corporate goals.
- *Autonomy*. An effective marketing organization empowers employees in traditionally powerless positions and transforms them into value-added corporate brainpower. Providing these individuals with the appropriate authority to make decisions and commit resources without recourse to higher-ups then creates the space and place within an organization for all employees to do their jobs well. Such empowerment also instills pride and enhances trust and commitment, while encouraging the intelligent exercise of defined prerogatives at every level.
- *Team Support*. To increase corporate and marketing productivity, the effective marketing organization establishes flexible, multi-functional teams to explore new challenges while also allowing for self-initiated projects.
- *Training*. To improve job performance and encourage individual growth, effective marketing organizations offer appropriate training, access to corporate support and information and a range of challenging cross-training opportunities.

The Bottom Line

Financial services companies have been slow to recognize the critical importance of incorporating strong marketing-driven influences into every aspect of their business mix. As competitive pressures within the financial services industry continue to grow, however, financial services organizations are increasingly becoming more favorably disposed to giving the marketing discipline a prominent place at the management table. Firms in many industry sectors are beginning to restructure their organizations to make integrated marketing initiatives part of the corporate culture and employ a range of additional tools and techniques that can help increase sales, productivity and retention.

Is your organization an extraordinarily effective marketing organization?

3

A Marketing Compass

What we now call marketing began long before the name was coined. In the mid–1800s, traveling salesmen camouflaged worthless tonics in fancy bottles in order to peddle their snake oil to a gullible public. Early successes led to the belief that the right marketing approach could help produce favorable results in virtually any business situation. The result was a proliferation of new promotional applications—some ethical, many not. Over the years, companies of all types have spent billions of dollars to figure out what works and what does not, and marketing has evolved from its rather crude beginnings to encompass a plethora of sophisticated strategic and tactical techniques.

Over the years, the consumer products industry has led the marketing charge and created marketing best practices that helped spawn consumer giants. Meanwhile, most financial services firms are being dragged, kicking and screaming, into the era of sophisticated marketing.

Putting the Customer First

Peter Drucker was an academic and marketing luminary whose writings greatly influenced the thinking of marketing practitioners. Over fifty years ago, Drucker developed the concept of a customer-centric marketing approach and coined the term *customer defined value*.

This concept has since become an integral part of marketing literature and the guiding principle of modern marketing. The following statements, paraphrased from Drucker's extensive writings, reflect his fundamental mandate that "the customer's interests must come first":

- The only valid definition of business purpose is to create a customer.
- What the business thinks it is producing is not as important as what customers think they are buying; what customers consider to be of value is decisive.
- Every business has only two basic functions: marketing and innovation.
- Marketing is your whole business as seen from the customer's point of view.

While the concept is straightforward and easily articulated, most financial services organizations have found it difficult to implement meaningful customer-centric practices. Some of the most common obstacles have included a product-push mentality, a focus on short-term profitability, under-investment in marketing activities and the lack of solid market intelligence about the needs and wants of target markets.

However, in the future the most successful financial services organizations will be those that make Drucker's principles their own through client-centric and creative applications.

The Advancing State of Financial Services Marketing

The financial services industry has lived on the edge of turmoil for the last couple of decades. As a result, the industry has undergone significant structural changes. Further, in response to increased competitive pressures, many financial services organizations have also become aware of the need to reconsider their traditionally conservative, undisciplined and very expensive marketing practices. They realize that future success depends on developing and refining market-driven processes.

Our observations suggest that the more progressive financial services organizations are currently experiencing an intellectual and practical transition that has caused them to elevate the role of marketing within their firms.

Marketers traditionally concentrated their efforts on implementation initiatives while management dealt with the broader strategic issues that affected the firm's future. The advent of customer-driven marketing and the attendant need to understand market-driven influences caused management to recognize the importance of accurate, timely and in-depth marketing intelligence—especially concerning customers, markets, distribution channels, products and services—to the strategic process. To address these new needs, marketing directors began to play an increasingly important role in the strategic planning and decision-making process.

As a result, the very nature of the marketing function in many firms is changing dramatically. This new breed of marketing professional now works closely with senior management on important strategic projects that will impact the entire organization and shape its future success. These projects include the development and refining of

- the firm's mission statement and key messages
- business objectives and value propositions
- statements of the company's relevant differentiation and competitive advantages.

At the same time, however, the status quo still prevails in many financial services organizations that have not yet recognized the benefit of adding sophisticated marketing to their business mix. Some organizations continue to squander valuable marketing resources on advertising campaigns focused on increasing visibility or gaining "share of voice." In addition, the persistent problem of differentiating marketing from sales still remains largely unresolved in many of these organizations.

The Bottom Line

The financial services industry is currently going through a dramatic marketing transformation. As effective financial services marketing evolves to a cross-functional, multidisciplinary activity, successful firms will create a culture of customer orientation throughout the organization and incorporate advocacy for customer welfare in all corporate decision making. Unfortunately, this puts the goalpost a significant distance away for far too many financial services firms.

The challenge for management is to provide the leadership required to displace the status quo and create a culture of opportunity. To compete effectively, financial services firms must become attuned to the market and adopt (and maintain) a market-driven focus on an organization-wide basis. Those firms that successfully develop a customer-oriented culture will be rewarded with enhanced opportunities for innovation, improved performance and incremental profitability.

4

Seeking the Outstanding Marketing Director

Marketing directors shoulder a significant amount of responsibility and play a key role in helping their companies create relevant marketplace differentiation. Successful marketing directors aggressively seek unique opportunities and champion the unconventional in their quest to conceive and implement appropriately timed alternatives to status quo marketing solutions.

Having worked with some of the best marketing directors in the financial services industry, I will borrow a page from David Letterman and provide a Top Ten List of the qualities a financial services organization should look for in a new marketing director. Here are the traits that I believe make up the DNA that distinguishes an Outstanding Marketing Director (OMD) from all the rest.

10. *Responsive*: OMDs do a lot of listening to obtain the constant feedback they need to keep in touch with customer attitudes,

track changes in behavior, identify trends and spot emerging customer needs.

9. *Insightful*: OMDs understand that people crave positive change. In spite of repeated admonitions about everyone's resistance to change, OMDs realize that people always hope for something better and believe that new concepts and approaches will have a positive impact. They understand that customers buy expectations, not products or services.

8. *Pragmatic*: OMDs are realistic thinkers. The optimistic nature of many marketing professionals can create serious damage. Positive thinking too often becomes wishful thinking that works against the best interests of the organization. Successful OMDs couple a positive attitude with pragmatic thinking and match vision with realistic action plans.

7. *Creative*: OMDs are both left- and right-brain thinkers. While the essence of any marketing director's position is creativity, OMDs must also be analytical. The most successful marketing directors create measurable goals, establish benchmarks and employ quantitative evaluation to justify current efforts.

6. *Decisive*: OMDs are leaders. Most marketing departments suffer from a lack of leadership and a surfeit of management. Managers do things right; leaders do the right things. While both roles are critical, it is the leader who raises the marketing role from a perfunctory staff function to a driver of corporate success.

5. *Informed*: OMDs combine (a) an in-depth knowledge of their company's offerings and operations with (b) comprehensive industry knowledge and a keen awareness of competitive and market forces. The ability to analyze the nuances of their organization's business against the competitive landscape provides the perspective needed to identify and evaluate opportunities, articulate a clear strategic vision and develop effective market positioning.

4. *Committed*: OMDs strongly believe that (a) it's better to do it right the first time and (b) lack of imagination and commitment are the only limitations on what can be accomplished. They are driven not just to understand the mission, goals and plans, but to internalize them.

3. *Efficient*: OMDs are process driven. They avoid repeating the errors of the past by implementing a structure that enables them to

capitalize on lessons learned, systematize the workflow and handle repeat situations with fluency.

2. *Resourceful*: OMDs skillfully orchestrate internal and external resources. Realizing that marketing budgets are always constrained, they find creative ways to utilize available resources to increase capabilities, leverage budgets and achieve ambitious goals.

1. *Risk Takers*: OMDs are willing to go out on a limb to maintain their independent perspective. While acknowledging the importance of marketing basics, they understand that cutting-edge and memorable marketing expressions lack precedents. They realize the need to escape from the unproductive box of pedestrian thinking in order to create and implement differentiated marketing programs.

The Bottom Line

Marketing directors in financial service organizations face unprecedented opportunities and challenges. It takes the skills and dedication of an outstanding marketing professional to help an organization distinguish itself and develop meaningful value propositions that will resonate in the marketplace. While the penalties for not creating relevant differentiation have always been harsh, the speed with which it is now imposed is faster than ever before.

II
STRATEGIC PLANNING

5

Strategic Strategy

There was a time, perhaps not so long ago, when the phrase "marketing strategy" referred to a well-researched and considered approach designed to help an organization create a sustainable competitive advantage. Now the word "strategy" is often little more than an overused buzzword. We have the strategic marketing plan, the strategic corporate positioning, the strategic advertising campaign, the strategic direct mail program, the strategic online marketing campaign and more. I bet there is even someone somewhere who has labeled their work strategic strategy. It is often difficult to recognize the genuine strategy from the faux.

Strategic Origins

In its purest form, strategy is the art of creating competitive advantage over your adversaries knowing that your adversaries are trying to do the same thing to you. If that sounds a bit militaristic, it is. The word "strategy" comes from the Greek word for "generalship" or "the art of the commander and chief." It is the planning that enables one party to triumph over another. The earliest known reference to an individual responsible for strategic planning appeared in Sun Tzu's *The Art of War,* written in China 2,500 years ago.

Business Planning Becomes Strategic

After World War II, many American businesses experienced phenom-
enal growth. These increasingly complex organizations also brought
new management problems. In response, management turned to
sophisticated accounting techniques to develop plans that placed
budgetary parameters around specific marketing activities. These
so-called "strategic plans" were more an exercise in immediate control
than an expression of strategic intent. Not surprisingly, this approach
did not provide the help management needed and the pendulum soon
swung in the totally opposite direction. The next major trend in
strategic planning focused on long-range planning rather than budgetary micro-management. Thereafter, it did not take long for companies to realize the folly of trying to predict events as far as five years
out. It was soon time for another approach.

Faced with the reality of two failed industry-wide approaches to
strategic marketing planning, corporate America turned to the professional consulting community for guidance. Consulting firms gladly
obliged with a variety of strategic planning approaches that brought
them business and marketplace recognition. Many of these approaches
involved innovative quantitative planning models that efficiently
processed corporate and market data but did nothing to reflect a
company's individual corporate culture or management expertise. The
problems inherent in a strategic planning process that excluded instinct
and other qualitative factors soon became manifest. These strategic
plans—developed by consultants for implementation by management—spawned largely ineffective processes. Management was again
prepared for new approaches to strategic marketing planning.

Enter the academicians, armed with a plethora of new concepts,
models and strategic planning guidelines that drew on the insights and
lessons accrued during sixty years of strategic thinking and failed
experiences. Among those who rushed in to fill the breach were
thought leaders like David Aaker, Peter Drucker, John Kenneth
Galbraith, Gary Hamel, Philip Kotler, Henry Mintzberg and Michael
Porter. Their strategic marketing approaches have evolved into a new
school characterized by concepts as varied as raising quality, lowering
prices, erecting barriers to entry and focusing on building customer

satisfaction. The great diversity of approach and opinion rejuvenated strategic marketing planning and brought it into the real world. As a result, strategic planning has become an essential part of a marketers' tool kit.

Now corporate leaders have the flexibility to consider a wide range of strategic approaches in their quest to develop customized strategic plans that suit their companies' strengths and objectives. Modern planning theory recognizes that a successful strategy must reflect not only a company's unique capabilities and characteristics, but also the realities of the marketplace. To this end, many companies use the SWOT technique, one of the oldest and most effective strategic tools. This technique helps marketers to systematically assess their corporate Strengths, Weaknesses, Opportunities and Threats as a preamble to successful strategic marketing planning.

The Bottom Line

Properly conceived and executed, marketing strategy can provide the framework that can help an organization focus its organizational capabilities, talent and energy on those initiatives that will create competitive advantage. From its shaky beginnings, strategic marketing planning has developed into a flexible, sophisticated discipline. However, marketing strategy is too important to be the sole province of financial marketers. It is incumbent on every financial services leader to become a student of contemporary strategic marketing thinking.

6

The Starting Point

While the financial services industry increasingly acknowledges the value of developing a strategic plan, it has not reached a consensus on how to approach the planning process. We believe that the starting point for the development of an effective strategic plan is the definition of a business's role in the marketplace. A clear business definition facilitates the planning process by providing a focal point for corporate decisions concerning target markets, product offerings, competitive standings and appropriate marketing activities. How management answers the question, "What business(es) are we in?" can have a significant effect not only on the company's strategic planning, but also on its ultimate success.

Lessons from the Past

Theodore Levitt, the Harvard University marketing guru, believed that the greatest threat to a company's growth was not market saturation, but rather the failure to create a strategy that properly defines the organization's driving purpose. In *Marketing Myopia*, published in 1983, Levitt offers the railroads as an object lesson of what can happen to an industry that loses its sense of direction and purpose. Levitt illustrates that the railroads did not stop growing because the need for passenger or freight transportation declined or because others (e.g., trucks and airplanes) moved in to usurp the railroads' transportation mandate. The truth is that the railroads allowed others to take their customers because they adopted a product-driven, rather than a customer-driven, strategy and failed to respond to the needs of the marketplace. They assumed that they were in the railroad business rather than the transportation business.

Twenty years earlier, Jacques Barzun had also studied the railroad industry and pinned its demise on a myopic nature that prevented it from staying attuned to the marketplace and focusing on consumer needs and wants. In *Trains and the Minds of Men,* Barzun wrote, "I grieve to see the most advanced physical and social organization of the last century go down in shabby disgrace for lack of the same comprehensive imagination that built it up. The void is the will of companies to satisfy the public by inventiveness and skill."

Looking to the Future

Examples of the disconnect between industry focus and customer demand abound in today's society. Consider the high-profile efforts of the record industry to protect their rights from the electronic music pirates. They desperately fought to maintain the traditional music industry infrastructure, when they should have focused on how to best adapt to the evolving technology and the needs of the marketplace. They had only to consider the fate that befell those Hollywood studios that did not recognize the growing impact of television and continued to follow a movie-oriented rather than an entertainment-oriented strategy. Like the railroads, they failed because they were product oriented rather than customer needs oriented.

There are, however, companies in many different industries that are responding to changing times by redefining their business objectives and developing strategies that reflect those new business definitions. For example, many copier companies have morphed into automated office systems organizations, while some telephone companies are recasting themselves as communications-based systems firms.

Financial Services Applications

The financial services industry continues to undergo a dramatic transformation fueled by

- evolving economic and market conditions
- the development of new products, services, distribution channels and competition
- the increased public awareness made possible by advances in information technology.

The reactions of different firms have varied greatly as they seek to adjust to the many changing factors that influence their businesses. The important thing financial services firms should not lose sight of, however, is that the definition of their individual businesses should drive their marketplace approach—not the other way around. The relevant cause and effect variables are shown in the following table:

Influence	Business Definition	Marketing Result
Customer behavior	Orientation and objectives	Definition of market boundaries
Organizational strength/weakness	Relevant differentiation from competitors	Organization/product positioning
Resource availability	Innovative solutions	Differentiated product/ service offerings

The question of business definition is relevant, not only when a major corporate event occurs, but also every time a financial product or service is

- introduced or discontinued
- directed to new customers or distribution channels
- acquired or divested.

The Bottom Line

Financial service firms committed to creating effective strategy should discard convention. They should first identify the consumer groups and consumer functions they serve and then define the most effective and relevant role for their businesses. This consumer-driven focus will provide the best strategic starting point and serve as the context for responding to all other strategic questions.

7

You Can Plan on It

"If you don't know where you're going any road will take you there." This old proverb makes a lot of sense. The best way to conserve resources and optimize results in any endeavor is to set a goal and then follow a well-researched and carefully plotted route to get there. This is especially true for financial marketers who have limited budgets to create marketing initiatives that will achieve ambitious corporate objectives. A carefully executed marketing plan serves as the blueprint for the creation of market-driven marketing programs.

Identify Your Planning Profile

Experience shows that an organization's attitude to the planning process and the importance generally placed on it fit into one of the following categories.

- *Passive*. Organizations that don't actively engage in marketing planning are defaulting on their obligation to actively promote the growth of their organizations. By accepting the status quo as their blueprint for the future, these organizations are fated to be reactors, rather than market leaders.
- *Regressive*. Well-established organizations are often satisfied to live on the glory of yesteryear. In these organizations, planning

focuses on making sure that everything is done just as it has always been done.

- *Preservationist.* Organizations that have reached a reasonable level of success often focus on maintaining their current status rather than going on to the next level. They resist any attempts to rock the boat and avoid any changes that will be disruptive to their current environment.
- *Progressive.* Growth-oriented organizations that seek market leadership explore all possible approaches and opportunities to create the relevant marketplace differentiation that will lead to future success.

One Size Does Not Fit All

"Plans are nothing; planning is everything," said General Dwight D. Eisenhower. Because the planning process is so important, we recommend that every organization take the time to develop their own planning style and make it a part of their culture.

Far too many organizations try to conform their marketing plans to pro forma templates borrowed from textbooks or colleagues. This approach usually produces a well-meaning academic document, when what is needed is a compelling discussion of how to effectively implement marketing initiatives that will enable the organization to most cost-effectively achieve its goals.

The most important building block for a successful planning process is the organization's own mission statement. It provides an unswerving focal point and can serve as a litmus test to determine the appropriateness, relevance and feasibility of issues and initiatives proposed during the planning process.

In far too many organizations, however, the mission statement has lost its viability as a guiding light and a planning tool. Why? Because the organization has hijacked the mission statement for use primarily as a public relations vehicle. The result generally is a generic statement that does not address the firm's unique culture and values. While this approach may help PR efforts, it does nothing to reflect an organization's culture, values and focus or inform its marketing efforts.

Research: The Foundation of the Marketing Planning Process

An effective marketing plan must reflect not only an organization's own capabilities and objectives, but also the realities of the market-place. Therefore, the marketing planning process begins with a focused internal and external information-gathering initiative that explores the following:

- *Market Environment.* The economic, regulatory and industry conditions and trends that will impact marketing efforts and market receptivity.
- *Competitors.* Marketplace positioning and tactical initiatives of companies with the same, similar or tangential products and services for the same target markets.
- *Customers.* Demographic characteristics, purchase behaviors and other relevant information on current and past accounts that will provide insights on best targets for future prospecting.
- *Target Markets.* Segment characteristics, receptivity to offerings, cost of entry and competitive pressures.
- *Profitability.* Broken out by markets, distribution channels and products/services.
- *Marketing Accountability.* Applicable benchmarks and success criteria.
- *Marketplace Opportunities.* Feasibility studies, identification of unmet market needs, identification of dissatisfaction with existing providers, etc.

Marketing Planning Pitfalls to Avoid

Here are some commonly heard statements that indicate that the planning process is doomed to failure.

- *"We'll worry about what we want to do later."* Without the requisite research, analysis and prioritization, this "ready, fire, aim" approach results in a hastily assembled plan that does not reflect the organization's needs, resources, objectives or marketplace circumstances. With no pragmatic, proactive planning, the organization will most probably find itself playing catch up and reacting to marketplace events and competitive innovations.

- *"Just find out what the sales force wants."* Financial services marketers are too often over-influenced by the sales force, a body with goals and priorities that are generally not in total alignment with those of the organization as a whole.
- *"We don't need customer research, we know what we need to do."* The fundamental goal of good marketing is to find the best way to make a connection with the target market. Yet numerous organizations approach marketing planning from the inside out rather than from the outside in. Marketing approaches that don't reflect the customer's perspective will most likely be ignored by the customer.
- *"If we try to set priorities now, we'll never get this plan approved."* An effective plan must contain clear directives to allocate limited resources to those areas that can potentially produce the greatest returns.
- *"Our job is just to get new customers in the door."* A plan that does not include up sale, cross sale and resale initiatives to create incremental business from existing customers is not making best use of the dollars spent to acquire those customers.

The Bottom Line

The marketing planning process provides an organization with the opportunity to set goals and plot a course that will help it achieve a differentiated market leadership position. A carefully researched, customized marketing plan can, if systematically implemented, serve as the backbone for an organization's marketing activities. It is worth every bit of the effort that it takes to get it right—the first time.

8

The Best Laid Plans

"When we fail to plan, we are planning to fail." This old adage is particularly applicable to the marketing planning process. Far too many large financial services organizations that depend on interdepartmental cooperation fail to take advantage of a marketing plan's ability to serve as a roadmap for favorably positioning the organization and its products and services.

Over the years, we have reviewed many marketing plans. Some take a minimalist approach and consist of little more than a mission statement and a budget. Others have more weight—but often, unfortunately, not much more substance—and come packaged in impressive tabbed binders with prolific exhibits. In some cases, marketing directors admit that they do not consider the production of these documents an integral part of the marketing process, but rather just an annual exercise that must be endured to please management and meet a deadline. Each year they enthusiastically present a new plan with the objective of making everyone feel good. Then it gets filed away. What a shame.

An effective marketing plan can help a company meet corporate objectives, most importantly by engendering understanding and support among all the stakeholders in corporate success. Therefore, the need to communicate with and get buy-in from diverse constituencies should drive every decision made during the creation of the marketing plan.

Tips for Developing an Effective Marketing Plan

We have, over time, developed a few guidelines that can help facilitate the development of an effective marketing plan.

Tip #1: There is no single right way to create a marketing plan. The correct format is the one that best meets a corporation's specific needs. Companies that slavishly follow a one-size-fits-all textbook template often end up with a plan that includes an elaborate table of contents and lots of data, but fails to effectively communicate and persuade.

Tip #2: Coalesce the readers' thinking around common goals. Effective marketing plans should provide a realistic discussion of the company's problems and opportunities, as well as its target markets, competitive environment and the strategic and tactical approaches that will create competitive advantage.

Tip #3: Brevity can be the key to a successful plan. A clear and concise articulation of the major issues and the recommended marketing approaches is the best way to engage readers. Mark Twain aptly said, "I didn't have time to write you a short letter, a long one must suffice." Those committed to producing a convincing marketing plan, however, will not only provide the necessary supporting data, but also take the time to create a compelling and focused narrative.

Tip #4: Two (or more) plans can be better than one. Successful consumer products companies with multiple product or service lines avoid confusion by preparing individual marketing plans for each line. Each individual plan articulates the proposed strategy to achieve growth and profitability in its respective product area. These multiple plans, with detailed background information and specific initiatives for each product/service line, provide convincing evidence that marketing is looking to make a buck rather than pass the buck.

Tip #5: Know and respect established boundaries and limitations. It is neither practical nor constructive to propose initiatives that necessitate changing or reversing unalterable policies, procedures and practices or other givens in the organization or in the marketplace. A more pragmatic approach reinforces the plan's credibility and maintains focus on the clear articulation of the plan.

Making the Marketing Plan Part of the Corporate Culture

A well-planned and well-executed communications program is critical to the successful implementation of a marketing plan. In fact, there is a point at which improving the quality of plan communications may be more effective than improving the quality of the plan.

Too many marketing directors make the mistake of presenting their marketing plans as a fait accompli. A successful marketing plan communications program focuses instead on eliciting—and maintaining—the support and buy-in of the entire organization.

Getting buy-in: A series of well-orchestrated, interactive kickoff meetings is generally an effective way to engage functional groups. These meetings can be used not only to introduce the goals, strategies and tactics outlined in the plan, but also to get input and foster understanding that the plan's ultimate success will be determined by cooperation across departmental lines. Senior management should participate in all these meetings to affirm the importance of these activities to the future of the corporation.

Maintaining momentum: It is important to utilize every opportunity available to keep the entire organization focused on the successful implementation of the marketing plan. Marketing plan information and updates can be included in newsletters, bulletins and meetings— not only at regularly scheduled meetings such as sales conferences and board meetings, but also at orientation, training and departmental review sessions.

The Bottom Line

The marketing plan is an important but too often underutilized tool that can play a key role in helping financial services organizations achieve their goals. A rigorous marketing planning process—from research through plan development and implementation—provides an excellent opportunity to

- gain important insights concerning the marketplace environment and your company's position in it
- explore critical issues and their attendant problems and opportunities
- clearly define marketing objectives
- develop integrated strategic and tactical solutions that will help your company gain competitive advantages and increase market share
- establish a singular marketing vision and foster teamwork among different functional areas so that key employees understand how they can help the company achieve important marketing and profitability objectives.

9

A Mission Possible

The mission of this chapter is to explain the essence and importance of the corporate mission statement. Many organizations discount the value of a mission statement, and several even take pride in not having one. A good mission statement can, however, contribute to an organization's success by providing a clearer focus for all corporate activities and creating clarity and consensus around the company's objectives and capabilities.

A Statement of Corporate Personality

Organizations, like individuals, possess a set of identifying characteristics that impact how they are viewed by the outside world. Unlike individuals, however, organizations consist of a number of people who simultaneously interact with a number of constituencies. A mission statement helps orchestrate these multiple interactions by providing a common point of reference for organizational unity. A well-crafted document clearly articulates what the organization stands for and where it's headed, helps codify management thinking and can be influential in shaping and communicating the identity of an organization.

The history of Northwestern Mutual provides a time-tested exemplar of the value of promoting and following a well-understood,

clearly articulated mission statement. In 1888, Northwestern Mutual Life created *The Northwestern
Mutual Way*, an expression of the
guiding principles that the company
continues to use to measure their
corporate success. This corporate
credo has helped Northwestern
make consistent decisions, create
organizational unity and integrate
short- and long-range goals.

> **The Northwestern Mutual Way**
>
> *"The ambition of the Northwestern
> has been less to be large than to be
> safe; its aim is to rank first in benefits
> to policyowners rather than first in
> size. Valuing quality above quantity,
> it has preferred to secure its business
> under certain salutary restrictions
> and limitations rather than to write a
> much larger business at the possible
> sacrifice of those valuable points
> which have made the Northwestern
> pre-eminently the policyholder's
> Company."*

Tips for Developing an Enduring Mission Statement

It takes effort and commitment to create a statement that truly reflects
an organization's beliefs and goals. We have, over time, developed a few
important guidelines that can help facilitate the development of an
effective mission statement.

*Tip #1: Solicit input from key individuals throughout the com-
pany.* Experience shows that one of the most effective approaches is to
assign the job of crafting the mission statement to a group that includes
a diversity of representation and operates within an imposed but
realistic deadline.

Tip #2: Define the target audience. Mission statements can be
designed for general distribution or for a specific audience, such as
employees, customers, or shareholders. The target audience selected
will also help determine the length and visibility of the statement.

Tip #3: Determine what form and tone the statement should take.
Corporate objectives, as well as the needs and preferences of the target
audience, should drive this decision. Some organizations write a
straightforward statement of purpose, while others focus on conveying
their philosophy or code of ethics. Titles such as "This We Believe,"
"Our Way," "Corporate Goals," "Our Vision" and "Values We Share"
reflect the focus of a given mission statement and the priorities of the
organization.

Tip #4: Watch your language. The consistent use of carefully selected key words can facilitate the development of a focused mission statement. A review of numerous statements reveals repeated use of the following key words:

Best	Growth	Respect
Commitment	Individual	Responsibility
Communities	Innovation	Serve/Service
Customers	Leader/Leadership	Shareholders
Employees	Long-term	Strength
Environment	Mission	Success
Excellence	Performance	Team/Teamwork
Fair	Profit	Value/Values
Goal	Quality	Vision

Tip #5: Make it personal. Many approaching the creation of a mission statement for the first time often lean too heavily on their research into the mission statements of other companies. Admittedly, a review of what others have crafted can provide a valuable starting point. However, an effective mission statement must reflect the adopting corporation's true personality—its beliefs, culture and practices. It is, in effect, a valuable corporate asset that most companies choose to copyright.

The Bottom Line

It is not easy to create an effective mission statement that is truly reflective of the organization's beliefs and goals. It takes hard work and the carefully considered input of key individuals throughout the organization. However, a properly executed mission statement can provide meaningful rewards for the investment of time and effort. Any organization—large or small—that decides to operate without such a statement deprives itself of an important tool that can help it to achieve greater organizational focus.

10
What's the Big Idea?

Every now and then a major marketing idea comes along that revolutionizes the way that marketers approach their craft. Some simply set the stage for the next big idea, while the most influential have a significant impact that lasts for decades.

A Case in Point

In 1961, Rosser Reeves published *Reality in Advertising* and introduced marketers to the concept of the "Unique Selling Proposition" or USP. Reeves posited that product/service marketing created the greatest marketplace impact when it focused on the USP, the single aspect of the product/service that most significantly distinguished it from competitive offerings. The directive was simple: Identify the USP and then hammer it home—repeatedly.

Throughout the sixties and seventies, most effective product/ service advertising and promotion employed the USP approach. Then, some marketing experts took issue with this focus on a single differentiating factor of a product or service. They believed that effective marketing depended not on how your message described the product or service but rather on what impression your message made on the mind of the audience. Thereafter, "positioning" became the new marketing buzzword.

The two early proponents of positioning were the marketing thought leaders Al Ries and Jack Trout. Their 1981 groundbreaking book, *Positioning: The Battle for Your Mind*, was a direct response to the nonstop sensory assault that characterized the marketing of that time. The dramatic proliferation of marketing promotion for virtually all products and services had created unprecedented marketplace clutter.

The high priests of the advertising business, won over by the compelling logic of positioning, scurried to embrace this new concept. A marketing revolution was born. Now, decades later, positioning has evolved from a marketing buzzword to a marketing approach that is still extensively used—and frequently misused—in today's marketing environment.

The ABCs of Positioning

Positioning aims to orchestrate the image and perceptions of a given product or service so that it occupies the premier place in the customer's mind relative to competitive offerings. Effective positioning triggers conditioned selection responses when individuals are asked to choose the best brand in a particular product category. The ultimate goal is to have your product or service become virtually synonymous with its product category (e.g., people ask for a Kleenex rather than a tissue and make a Xerox instead of a copy). Similarly, ask people to name a brand of soft drink, soup or razor blades, and the most common answers will almost always be Coke, Campbell's and Gillette.

Brand prominence is especially important in product sectors where there are few, if any, distinguishing factors between competing brands. When competing brands in a product category are so similar, the advantage goes to the one that is favorably positioned in consumers' minds. It is the conditioned selection response produced by strong marketing positioning that motivates consumers to choose between close competitors such as Coke and Pepsi, Colgate and Crest, New York Life and MetLife or American Funds and T. Rowe Price.

Taking Aim

The old adage warns, "When you try to be all things to all people, you end up not being anything to anyone." In other words, the less something stands for the stronger it is.

Therefore, the first rule of effective positioning is to appeal directly to specific consumer attitudes, perceptions, needs and market trends. Position the product or service to stand for something that is intuitively appealing and then concentrate resources on reinforcing those attributes and perceptions.

Positioning campaigns that focus on a few strong attributes gain prominent positions in the minds of consumers far more effectively than more broad-based approaches. Over time, marketers have adopted, adapted and expanded positioning concepts in an effort to find differentiated ways to gain a unique position in the minds of their target markets. The result has been a broad range of positioning strategies and approaches based on, to name only a few, low price, quality, originality, distribution channels, competitive excellence or a specific appeal to a target market. Companies also continually revise, reinvent or expand their positioning to appeal to the arrival of a new natural or created niche.

Positioning is a mind game, and the objective is to make a differentiated appeal that conforms to the way people think and react to the information they continually encounter.

The Bottom Line

Positioning brings to the forefront a basic concept that underlies all good marketing: Perception becomes reality. Positioning, therefore, focuses on the logic and processes that the human mind employs to make decisions in the midst of the overabundance of choices and other stimuli that confront us every day. Therefore, how a product or service is perceived (read: positioned) versus its competition is a key determinant of marketplace success. However, marketers must never lose sight of the fact that success follows truth. To be most successful, you must always be able to deliver—or hopefully over-deliver—what you are promising the marketplace.

11
New and Improved

We often tell clients that their future success depends on their ability to create relevant differentiation in a highly competitive marketplace. The challenge, therefore, is to create innovative products, services and approaches that will help create competitive advantage.

The Value of Innovative Approaches

Organizations that eschew innovation and simply try to beat the competition at their own game soon learn that going head-to-head with competitors generally provides only modest incremental gains. Success, in the form of rapid growth and high margins, comes most often to those organizations that understand the value of innovation and look beyond current competitive practices. These companies adopt a new perspective to find financial products and services that provide significant customer benefits by filling unmet marketplace needs.

Merrill Lynch offers a classic example of this type of innovative thinking.

- *Background*. The year is 1975. Since the Glass–Steagall Act mandated a separation between banking and investment activities, investors held their uninvested assets in bank accounts and transferred funds to their brokerage accounts each time they made an investment. Then the mutual fund industry created money market funds, triggering a mass transfer of funds from low-interest banking accounts to these new funds that paid market rates. This run on the bank soon brought the word "disintermediation" into common usage as banks reeled from the loss of these relatively inexpensive assets. Brokerage firms also felt pain from the loss of float from "free balances."

- *Merrill Lynch's response.* Merrill created the central asset account, marketed under the name Cash Management Account® (CMA®). This revolutionary new product combined an investment account, an automatic sweep that placed cash balances in an interest-bearing account, a debit card and a credit line secured by the underlying investment account. It even offered FDIC deposit insurance. It was a marketplace coup. This one-stop shopping approach made life much easier for both brokers and their clients. As a result, it enhanced both client loyalty and broker productivity. At the same time, competitors were caught flatfooted—without either a comparable product or the technology to implement one. Merrill Lynch had a significant leader's advantage. By the time other brokerage firms were able to create similar offerings, Merrill Lynch had reaped the rewards of innovation (i.e., a significant market share and annual profits of more than $1.5 billion attributable to CMA activity alone).

A New Age of Possibilities

More liberal regulations have widened the universe of opportunities and strategies available to financial services organizations. The range of possibilities is now constrained only by their vision, creativity and willingness to build a culture of innovation. Sometimes an organization's biggest obstacles are the limits of its own vision and its unwillingness to plunge into the unknown. Changing this mindset is a challenge that can test an organization's mettle and determine its ability to move forward.

While innovation invariably entails certain risks, maintaining the status quo can often be riskier in the long run. Those in power, however, are often stalwart defenders of the status quo, as evidenced by the following historical quotes:

Pasteur's germ theory is ridiculous fiction.
          —Pierre Pachet, Professor of Physiology (1872)

Heavier than air flying machines are impossible.
          —Lord Kevin, President of the Royal Society (1895)

This "telephone" has no inherent value—it cannot be seriously considered as a means of communications.
                    —Western Union memo (1876)

Who the hell wants to hear actors talk?
          —H. M. Warner, Warner Brothers (1927)

The mantra of innovation is "If at first you don't succeed . . . " Interestingly, lessons learned from failures often reside in an organization's consciousness longer then lessons learned from success. Organizations also find that the innovation process itself often teaches them important lessons about their own businesses and the marketplace.

Embracing Innovation

Ideas are the currency of financial services innovation. Visionary organizations encourage a new idea flow through a process of continual discussion, analysis and testing. These organizations understand that innovation is the key to creating marketplace differentiation and winning competitive advantage. As a result, they focus first on creating new strategic opportunities, developing new or reconfigured financial products and services that leverage these opportunities and then on finding the appropriate marketplace for these innovative offerings.

The leading companies in a given market sector are those companies that have regularly overcome the resistance to change. Names like IBM, Google, Microsoft, Procter & Gamble and Macintosh immediately come to mind. The innovation imperative is compelling. Once your organization experiences it, there's no going back.

The Bottom Line

Over the years, organizations have tried several approaches to innovation with varying degrees of success. Larger organizations often create dedicated Research & Development departments charged with supplying a steady stream of breakthroughs. Smaller financial services firms usually rely on their internal management cadre to mine their own experience and creativity for innovative ideas and insights. However it is done, it is important for all organizations to have an innovation process. Any organization that is content to follow its competitors will always be just one of the pack and will continually find itself playing catch up as the competition moves forward.

12

In the Beginning

Financial services marketing directors experience their greatest occupational high when they are able to realize their vision of bringing a product or service innovation to market. The dream of every marketing director is to develop and implement the offering that will generate incremental sales, enhance profitability and help their company achieve a leadership position. Unfortunately, very few get the opportunity to fulfill that dream and experience the same euphoria that great inventors like Benjamin Franklin or Thomas Edison must have felt.

We have actively monitored the financial marketplace for a considerable time and have determined that the failure rate of innovative financial products and services can run in excess of 80 percent. Despite these odds, the search for the next big idea lives in the hearts and minds of almost every worthy marketing director.

A Cluttered Marketplace

Only a few decades ago, the vast majority of new financial products and services introduced into the marketplace were successful. In today's cluttered competitive environment, however, most financial product and service categories have matured and are overrepresented. Now, to become a marketplace success, a new product usually has to take market share from already established brands.

Financial product and service categories have become so saturated that market structures exhibit what economists call monopolistic competition. This apparent oxymoron describes a market characterized by intense price competition, the lack of a single dominant brand and competitive differentiation based primarily on brand perception rather than performance.

Orchestrating a Successful Product Debut

The activities surrounding the introduction of a new product or service are as important as its design or pricing. Experienced marketers create well-planned and effectively orchestrated product debut campaigns that include the following:

- Pre-launch activities consisting of both marketplace initiatives that build anticipation and interest and internal activities that generate enthusiasm and support for the forthcoming launch.
- Launch activities that build visibility and momentum.
- Post-launch activities that sustain the interest and momentum and serve as the foundation on which the firm can build an ongoing, cumulative marketing process.

There is a high cost associated with new product failures. We have done a number of autopsies on failed financial product and service introductions and have identified the following key issues as the major drivers of success or failure for new financial products and services:

- *Positioning and Messaging.* Customers buy expectations, not products and services, and always hope for new approaches that offer promise and fulfillment. Market messages that address these customer preferences are more likely to resonate in the marketplace.
- *Naming.* A good name can serve as a marketplace banner that generates greater visibility and acceptance. A name that

communicates benefits gets extra mileage and provides opportunities for more effective, lower-cost branding.

- *Sufficient Budget.* Most organizations underestimate introductory marketing costs. Our rule of thumb is to budget appropriately for an effective launch—then add more to the budget.
- *Market Intelligence.* We can learn a lot by examining the missteps of others and learning to anticipate problems. This is one area in which ignorance is definitely not bliss.
- *Relevant Marketplace Differentiation.* What many companies introduce as new products are actually near copies of competitors' offerings and represent more of the same to their target markets. With no competitive advantage, these companies need an exorbitant budget to generate excitement and buy even a modicum of success.
- *Distribution Strength.* Even the best products or services fail without adequate distribution and sales support. It is human nature to resist change and stay with what is known to work. Therefore, distribution channels require training, motivation and effective sales tools if they are to embrace a new product.
- *Brand Consistency.* Maintaining the confidence of its customers is critical to the success of any financial services organization. It is especially important, therefore, that the attributes and messages associated with any new product are strategically consistent with the sponsoring company's brand identity.
- *Reliable Marketplace Testing.* While consumer products marketers devote considerable resources to focus groups, we believe that this market testing technique is neither appropriate nor cost-effective for financial services marketing. Focused one-on-one interviews with distribution channel representatives and target market prospects provide a more in-depth and intimate reading of the financial needs and wants of the marketplace.

The Bottom Line

The vast majority of new financial product and service offerings are not successful. We have found that most of these costly disappointments can be attributed to the sponsoring organization's failure to

- identify and appeal to marketplace needs and wants
- provide relevant differentiation from more established brands
- effectively establish and motivate distribution channels
- create messaging that resonates with target markets
- live up to market expectations.

The pitfalls are obvious, and yet financial services marketers fall into them over and over again. As Walt Kelly's beloved comic strip character, Pogo the Possum, said, "We have seen the enemy, and he is us."

13

I Have an Idea

If you're in marketing you need to be creative. It's in the job description. Those in marketing are continually expected to produce new and innovative ideas on command for the corporate good.

For professional marketers, ideas represent solutions. I once had a plaque in my office that read, "When the answer is found it will be simple." The challenge is to take the complex, make it simple and then communicate it effectively.

The Quest for Good Ideas

In the 1940s James Webb Young, a seasoned advertising man, published a thin volume, entitled *A Technique for Producing Ideas,* based on a series of lectures he had given some years before. His pragmatic process still serves as the standard for the process of idea creation.

Mr. Young believed that, "An idea is nothing more or less than a combination of old elements." He believed that what distinguishes the creative mind is the ability to put things together in new ways, to find new relationships and juxtapositions. Creative people very seldom actually create. They simply reorganize, synthesize, reshuffle or combine things in a new way. As the great choreographer, George Balanchine, was fond of saying, "Only God creates, I just assemble very well."

Consider the case of Earle Dickson, who wanted to help his accident-prone wife. In 1920 Dickson took a piece of gauze, attached it to the center of a piece of tape and then covered the whole thing with crinoline to keep it sterile. Voila, the Band-Aid was born. Since then more than 100 billion have been sold.

To Think Like a Child

Creativity, then, is the ability to imagine new ways to use existing elements or ideas. The most creative thinkers are often children because their thinking has not yet been corrupted by adult society. They have no inhibitions and no preconceived ideas about what something means or how it should be used. Sigmund Freud created a technique called *free association* to help adults reconnect with this child-like way of thinking and more readily create new thoughts and ideas. Free association assumes that all thoughts and memories are arranged in a single associative network. It encourages people to begin with what they know about a problem, goal or question and then let the unfettered mind start creating a flow of ideas. Each idea, no matter how irrelevant or trivial, will trigger another idea until the solution appears.

To utilize free association to generate creative business ideas, marketers should begin with two key elements—specific subject knowledge and a clear, specific objective that is appropriate to the task. Framing the goal correctly is critical to success. For example, if Thomas Edison's objective had been to create a way to make the room brighter, he might have simply invented a sconce that would hold many more candles than a candlestick. However, his objective was to find a more sustainable source of light. To reach that goal, he had to think about other possible ways to illuminate a room—a thought process that led to the invention of the lightbulb. The clearer your objective, the more likely you will recognize the "Aha!" moment when it occurs.

What If . . . ?

Some of the best ideas are serendipitous or simply mistakes. For example, Charles Goodyear discovered vulcanization when he accidently dropped a glob of rubber and sulfur on a stove. Arguably there are people who have trained themselves to benefit from serendipity. Benjamin Franklin invented innumerable things, including the lightning rod, bifocals, a musical instrument, the odometer, and the Franklin stove, because he maintained an attitude that allowed him to recognize the implications of a lucky occurrence. Marketers have a responsibility to develop a more intuitive perspective by teaching themselves to recognize the possibilities of every occurrence, problem or idea, rather than letting its potential pass unrecognized.

Persistence is also an important part of the creative process. Far too often the best ideas are considered too different by many in the organization. Take Chester Carlson for example. His frustration with the slowness of the mimeograph machine and the cost of photography led him to invent a new electrostatic process, called xerography, which reproduced words on a page in just minutes. Carlson had a hard time finding investors for his new invention. He was turned down by IBM, General Electric, RCA and the U.S. Army. It took him eight years to find an investor, the Haloid Company, which later changed its name to the Xerox Corporation. The rest is history.

Another persistent and creative type was the prototypical marketing practitioner, a traveling salesman named King Gillette. On a trip around 1900, King dropped his straight razor, causing it to break in half. Looking at the pieces gave King an idea. After returning home to Boston, he glued the pieces back-to-back and then added housing and a handle to produce a more manageable and functional two-sided razor. King began marketing this "safety razor" with disposable blades. As hard as he tried, the first year he was only able to sell 51 razors. It was time for another idea. King began to give away the razors and then sold replacement blades with ample profit margin. The "loss leader" concept was born. By 1915, Gillette had produced 450,000 razors and sold more than 70 million blades. When World War I began in 1918, the Gillette Safety Razor Company provided every American soldier a field razor set paid for by the U.S. government.

The Bottom Line

Creativity is the essence of successful marketing. Creativity is a combination of deliberate idea generation, persistence and serendipity. Financial services organizations are increasingly dependent on creative marketing ideas to create visibility and competitive differentiation in a cluttered marketplace. Cultivating a well-defined and disciplined process for creativity is no longer a marketing option; it is a requirement.

14

Become a Marketing Hero

Let's face it. There are times when a product or service becomes difficult, if not impossible, to sell. Customers who were ready buyers in the past no longer have the same appetite. They have changed their preferences and express strong objections to the very offerings they previously embraced.

It's not difficult to be a marketing hero when offerings are well received in the marketplace. The real challenge for most marketers is to find a way to save the day when there is a difficult sales situation. Then the pressure is on, and the odds are not in their favor.

What Makes a Marketing Hero

While planning is always an important first step in any marketing activity, it is critical when dealing with distressed products/service offerings, recalcitrant markets, frustrated sales representatives and concerned management. In this overheated corporate environment, everyday marketers can become marketing heroes by exercising pragmatism and good critical judgment. To find the right answers for difficult challenges, marketers need to analyze the situation and determine which approaches are most likely to reap rewards commensurate with the needed expenditures. Only then is it time to make recommendations and commit resources.

Representative Marketing Challenges

Products and services become white elephants for a variety of reasons. Marketers need the wisdom and insight to determine when to take aggressive action and when it is best to let the markets take their course.

Scenario #1. A sudden shift in market conditions changes user sentiment. The trick to reviving a product or service that has become a white elephant is often a simple matter of cause and effect. A marketer must first understand why the product is not selling and then apply creative thinking to determine the best way to reposition the offering. The gas price crisis of 2008 offers a perfect example.

When gas prices skyrocketed, customers eschewed formerly popular gas guzzlers like Hummers and SUVs, and dealer inventories of these big vehicles ballooned to record numbers. Since the deterrent was not the price of the vehicle, traditional price discounts no longer worked. Dealers needed a creative approach to overcome buyers' objections and clear their showrooms. Some enterprising automakers directly addressed the cost-of-gas objection by offering free gas for a year or longer with every vehicle purchased. The strategy increased sales even though, at times, it probably represented less of a cost concession than the traditional year-end discount.

Scenario #2. A product or service is not addressing customer needs. Arm & Hammer Baking Soda had long been a pantry staple. As consumers' needs changed, however, the little yellow box became less and less important to their daily lives, and product sales went into a long-term slump. Then the company discovered that some customers placed an open box of baking soda in their refrigerators to suppress odors, and began to aggressively promote this use of its product. Soon, half of America had adopted this practice. The product now had a new purpose and sales levels increased dramatically.

This success sparked Arm & Hammer to seek other applications for its product. They then discovered that baking soda could minimize grease build up in kitchen drains, and launched another targeted campaign that again increased sales. Today, an Internet search reveals countless sites with offerings such as "thirty Baking Soda Tips," "Sixty-One Uses for Baking Soda" and "Resourceful and Ingenious Uses of Baking Soda." This formerly ne'er-do-well product is now a consumer darling.

Scenario #3. A product simply outlives its usefulness. One thing marketers need to consider is where a product or service is in its life cycle. Many an offering can be a good seller from the initial stages of growth and marketplace acceptance all the way through maturity. At some point, however, the declining phase of its life cycle sets in, and it becomes an increasingly hard sell. The buggy whip presents a classic marketing example of a sunset product that had seen its day and would never again have marketplace demand.

There are always current examples of products and services that are in the declining phase of their life cycle. To illustrate, as soon as the government announced the 2009 mandatory transition to digital TV, analog TV entered its sunset phase. While this is an obvious example, most times it is not easy to recognize when the declining phase of a product's life cycle has begun. Marketers must be vigilant in order not to squander resources trying to revive products or services that are doomed to extinction.

The Bottom Line

Products or services pass out of marketplace favor for different reasons. The marketer's challenge is to determine what is causing sales resistance and then determine the appropriate course of action. Does the situation require creative initiatives to reframe the offer and overcome objections, or should the product be better positioned to more directly meet consumer needs? It could be that the product is simply in the declining phase of its life cycle, in which case it is better to face reality and focus marketing resources on other offerings that will provide a better return on the marketing investment. Astute marketers that make the right choices and respond appropriately are destined to become marketing heroes.

III

TACTICAL IMPLEMENTATION

15
Brand Aid

Most prominent companies have long understood that a corporate brand is a valuable—albeit, intangible—business asset that must be carefully managed. There is no doubt that Coca Cola, IBM, CitiBank, Travelers and a host of other major corporations have been minding their brands for decades. Smaller financial services firms, however, have only recently begun to recognize the importance of developing a strong financial services brand.

What Is a Brand?

While positioning determines the mental and market space that a firm, product or service should occupy, branding delivers the unique perceptions that reinforce that positioning in the marketplace.

- *A brand is the face that a company projects in the marketplace.* It encompasses organizational attributes, corporate personality and brand symbols, as well as the perceptions held by the company's different constituencies.
- *A brand represents a company's reputation in the marketplace.* A strong brand engenders trust. It conveys the quality and reliability that people look for in a financial services provider.
- *A brand is a company's badge of distinction.* A strong brand can help create a differentiated corporate persona that enables a company to stand apart in an increasingly cluttered and competitive market.

Brand Benefits

Business literature has recently devoted a considerable amount of ink to the discussion of the significant benefits that a strong brand can impart to a corporation. At the macro level, a strong brand can help a firm achieve a leadership position within a market segment. On the micro level, a solid brand can impact customer familiarity, preferences and loyalty.

A strong brand communicates the corporate value proposition that helps an organization create relevant marketplace differentiation and competitive advantage. It can also help to significantly accelerate the sales process. Prospects who recognize and trust a brand will often set aside their routine skepticism and caution. They will, for example, forgo their normal due diligence, do less comparative shopping and act more quickly and confidently to make a positive buy decision.

Measuring the Value of a Brand

Brand equity is a measure of the predisposition of various constituencies to purchase or recommend a given brand. It consists of the audience's awareness of and familiarity with the brand and the images and perceptions they form by synthesizing the opinions, images and information available about the brand. Brand equity is, in effect, the power of a brand to create preference, satisfaction, loyalty and a positive association with successful products and services.

Since brand equity is highly qualitative, there is no single definitive measurement approach. David Aaker, one of the thought leaders in the area of brand equity, used the principles of consumer psychology to develop an approach that measures brand equity on four dimensions: brand awareness, perceived quality, brand associations and brand loyalty.

Brand Development and Management

Branding—the ongoing tasks associated with the creation of a strong market image and the effective management of market perceptions—is both an art and a science. Research studies, academic white papers and a robust branding agency industry are continually providing different approaches and new branding techniques to the marketplace.

There are, however, some basics that apply equally to branding a new company or revitalizing an existing brand.

Brand definition: What perceptions does the company want to create and maintain over the long term? What brand attributes would it like to have associated with the firm? For example:

- Does the company want to position itself as a specialist or have universal appeal?
- Does it want to move its brand up market or down market?
- Would brand extensions enhance or deteriorate its marketplace reputation?

Brand elements: If consistently and continually used, carefully developed visual and verbal symbols can reinforce the chosen brand attributes and serve as the company's marketplace signature. These elements include names (for the company and its products and services), benefit-driven marketing messages and a powerful design system that begins with a logo and color palette and then addresses all visual subjects and symbols, as well as graphic style and format.

The Bottom Line

Financial services firms of every size should now understand that their brand is a strategic asset that has a significant influence on long-term performance. The benefits of effective brand management accrue to an organization even though such branding concepts as trust, reputation, loyalty and emotion don't appear on the balance sheet.

In a cluttered environment where financial products and services are screaming for the attention that has become harder and harder to attain, a strong brand provides a shorthand for marketplace recognition and a corporate badge of distinction that paves the way for more immediate acceptance. With so much at stake, it is important that companies manage their brands and gain the maximum value that branding can provide.

Firms that do not make the effort to create a strong brand are missing the opportunity to take advantage of a powerful marketing tool that can help them effectively communicate with the marketplace and create long-term marketing success. However, careless branding is sometimes as harmful as no branding at all. Far too many firms create brand confusion by using verbal and visual brand symbols that send mixed messages to the marketplace.

Any firm that is not focused on managing and maximizing the value of its brand is missing an important opportunity.

16

Branding: Step One

One of the primary goals of the art of branding is to help a brand cut through the marketplace clutter and achieve visibility, credibility and acceptance. Naming is the important first step in the branding process. The better the name, the more potential it offers for effective, lower-cost branding that can help build visibility and brand recognition. The right name serves as the springboard for implementing an effective branding strategy and can play an important role in creating a strong emotional connection with the target market.

Unfortunately, there is no simple formula for creating a good name. There are, however, a few basic guidelines. A good name is both distinctive and memorable. It should be relevant to a company's industry and mission and reflect its corporate culture. A company should also consider if the name can be trademarked and if the corresponding URL is available. After that, there are a lot of options and approaches. The right name is the one that best suits your company and situation.

Naming Categories

Descriptive names do exactly as they say and describe what a company does. There is little doubt about what services you can obtain at businesses such as Asset Management Company, U.S. Bank, Insurance

Company.com, American Funds and Bank of the West. It is easy to cost-effectively promote these names because they explicitly address a marketplace need and there is no need for lengthy explanations. On the other hand, it is often quite difficult to gain trademark protection for these names because trademark laws preclude trademarking any word that is considered descriptive.

Names with provenance are most commonly derived from the names of individuals or places. Such names are distinctive and easy to trademark. The financial services business has a disproportionate share of companies branded with the names of founders and/or partners. A few prominent examples include Goldman Sachs, Cantor Fitzgerald, Dreyfus, Oppenheimer, Morgan Stanley and Brown Brothers Harriman. Many think that a family name personalizes an organization and offers customers the reassurance that credible individuals stand behind the corporate claims and representations.

Created names are often the last resort of marketers struggling to create a truly unique name that will confer immediate brand personality. When it works, a creative name can be a powerful corporate and legal asset. When it doesn't work, it can be a corporate millstone. To illustrate, in the 1920s, Duncan created the name Yo-Yo. Since then, the word has become a part of the lexicon as both the name of the original object and as a verb signifying up-and-down movement. More recent examples of names that have permeated the culture include Google and Yahoo!.

Associated names are essentially metaphors that relate the corporate name to a familiar reference that imparts favorable attributes to the brand. For example, names such as Passport Account and VISA convey immediate benefits that facilitate positive brand positioning.

A Car by Any Other Name

The automobile industry offers a perfect illustration of how companies use different approaches to naming to help motivate a purchase decision. European companies usually use descriptive names, and a glance at the trunk badge tells the buyer volumes—engine size, body style, fuel injection, length of wheelbase, etc.

In contrast, domestic automobiles use a variety of naming devices in the hopes of generating positive associations that will favorably influence prospective buyers. There are created names such as Alero, Integra and Xterra. Animal names are also popular. By using associated names such as Falcon, Viper, Firebird, Impala and Mustang, manufacturers try to represent some of the attractive characteristics of the vehicle. Model naming has even ventured into deep waters with the likes of Sting Ray and Barracuda. Just envision those high-powered Detroit marketing types brainstorming to arrive at the name Plymouth Duster. Were the runners up squeegee, mop and vacuum?

Heal Thyself

The pharmaceutical industry has shown that they understand the power of naming. Not long ago drugs were marketed primarily to doctors, and the names were simply recitations of their chemical compounds. To the consumer these names were uninformative, unpronounceable and sounded extraordinarily medical. Now that drugs are aggressively marketed directly to the consumer, a new era of savvy naming has recently blossomed. A pill is a pill, but give it an appealing name and it can become a gold mine. A created name like Viagra is distinctive without sounding like a drug. Benadryl, Sudafed and Claritin are easy to pronounce and remember, yet retain a scientific overtone. Names like Allegra, Boniva and Levitra are both distinctively named and lyrical. The pharmaceutical industry has repeatedly demonstrated that they understand how naming can help them increase their sales appeal within different target markets and make their pills so much easier to swallow.

Waiting in the Wings

The financial services industry has yet to fully focus on the importance of naming. Financial company names, much like those in the auto industry, have been, well, all over the lot. Historically, there have been descriptive names (e.g., Cash Management Account) and created names (e.g., SPDRs) that have been effective. In general, however, the industry has been woefully deficient in mastering the art of naming.

The Bottom Line

Evidence of the importance of naming is the proliferation of specialized name consultants in recent years. While the purported objective of these firms is always to create nomenclature that reflects their client's corporate culture, the results are far too often more influenced by their own culture and preferences.

A powerful name links the organization and its product/service offerings to the customer. A name is the most important element of the branding mix. It is a brand's calling card and communicates its key attributes and associations. It is well worth the upfront time and effort to create a naming system that will provide a logical and consistent foundation for all future marketing and communication efforts.

17
Write Right

At the dawn of the twentieth century, advertisers worked on the premise that customers were more likely to do business with a known entity. Therefore, companies used advertising simply to keep a company in the public eye. Then along came Claude Hopkins, a young man with a novel idea. He believed that advertising should actually sell a product and wrote copy that contained memorable slogans such as "Schlitz, the beer that made Milwaukee famous." As a result, he was soon hired by the Lord and Thomas Agency at the unheard of salary of $185,000 in 1908. Copywriting took on a new importance in the marketing world, and advertising would never again be the same.

Hopkins clearly knew how to appeal to the consumers of a century ago, but the question is whether he would succeed in today's text message and Blackberry world. Modern consumers are bombarded by unprecedented levels of visual and audio stimulation. The truth is that, in this environment, the basics of good copywriting espoused by Hopkins are more important than ever before. To be heard in the din of the marketplace and motivate the consumer to take the next step in the sales process, copy must have sufficient color, texture and emotion.

Headlines: Get Their Attention

You know what they say about first impressions. Well, the headline is where the copywriter can instantly create or suppress readership. Studies have shown that people are more likely to read shorter headlines and those that contain certain words and messages. People respond especially favorably to headlines that promise personal benefits, announce something new or arouse curiosity. A study conducted by the Yale University Psychology Department a number of years ago concluded that the ten most influential words in advertising are discovery, free, guarantee, health, love, money, new, safety, save and you.

Body Copy

Copywriting is an art, not a science. There is no right or wrong, no firm rules that guarantee success. However, there are guidelines that can help a creative idea find expression. For starters, it is important to have a powerful opening that will grab the readers' attention and get them involved. Thereafter, the copy must build a strong case for the superiority of its product or service. Each sentence and paragraph should lead inevitably to the next and ultimately to the call to action. The copy should speak directly and personally to the reader using simple words and short sentences and paragraphs. Like any other art form, good copywriting is entirely dependent on the skill of the creator. One successful copywriter offers the following advice: "If you want to be a well-paid copywriter, please your client. If you want to be an award-winning copywriter, please yourself. If you want to be a great copywriter, please your reader."

Long vs. Short

A recurring question is whether copy should be long or short. Again, there is no right answer. Both long copy and short copy have tested both well and poorly. It all depends on the situation and the skill of the copywriter. An old copywriters' adage from years gone by advises that "Copy is like a young lady's skirt. It should be long enough to cover all the essentials and short enough to make it interesting."

Looks Matter

The graphic presentation of an ad plays an important role in creating interest and readership. Graphic elements, like the copy they seek to enhance, should be simple, direct and striking, and create immediate interest. The selection of color, font, font size, illustrations and photographs will determine if the copy whispers or shouts, asks or demands.

The Bottom Line

A good copywriter, much like a good lawyer, is an advocate who builds a persuasive case for the client. Hard-working copy is the nucleus of effective marketing initiatives. It gets the readers' attention by relating to their wants and needs, makes a compelling case for the superiority of its subject product or service, and motivates the readers to take the carefully defined next step. Copy comes in all shapes, sizes and approaches. There is no right or wrong approach, just those that work and those that don't. That's why most successful copywriters employ a "ready, aim, fire" process. Ready takes only a few minutes. Fire takes only a few seconds. It's the aim part that is most critical, takes the most time and is most essential to the creation of great copy.

18
The Color of Marketing

In 1704, Sir Isaac Newton discovered that ordinary light is a mixture of hundreds, if not thousands, of different colors. However, artists declared that they needed only three primary colors—red, yellow and blue—to create any imaginable hue.

In 1802, Thomas Young made a discovery that reconciled these two seemingly contradictory claims. Young found that the human eye contains three sensors that correlate to the three pigments artists used to mix colors. Therefore, since our eyes have only three sensors with which to process the thousands of colors in the light spectrum, all colors that we see can be reduced to the three primary colors.

Today, sophisticated printing uses a four-color process that mixes black with the primary colors. The printing industry also has created terminology to facilitate communication between printers and marketing people about the various properties of a color—"hue" describes its purity, "strength" describes the saturation and "intensity" describes how *grey* it is (i.e., how much black has been added to the color).

Creating a Corporate Image

Corporations use a myriad of elements (e.g., name, symbols, colors) to establish a corporate brand identity that will distinguish the organization, its product/service offerings and its affiliated companies. The marketer's challenge is to create a consistent and competitively differentiated look and feel that will create visibility, recognition and, ultimately, brand loyalty.

Astute marketers understand that color can play an extremely important role in helping a company both express its positioning and corporate purpose and influence market perceptions and attitudes. The following are just a few examples of how companies have associated their organizations and/or their product/service offering with certain colors:

Company	Color(s)	Company	Color(s)
Campbell's	Red & White	Kodak	Yellow
Coca Cola	Red	National	Green
Fuji	Green	Pepsi	Red & Blue
Hertz	Yellow	Seven–Up	Green
ING	Orange	Visa	Blue & Gold

The vast amount of research conducted on the influence of color has proven that some colors have a greater tendency to generate pleasurable responses. Overall, the order of preferred colors is (1) blue, (2) red, (3) green, (4) purple, (5) orange and (6) yellow. From a gender perspective, both sexes prefer blue, with the runner-up being red for females and green for males. Research has also determined that younger people prefer pure, bright colors while softer, less intense tones appeal more to older people. In general, primary colors are favored and warm colors attract more attention.

Marketers must also consider the effects of synaesthesia when determining how to use color most effectively. The underlying concept is that color can have an emotional impact and evoke feelings concerning, for example, quality, strength, weakness, prestige, price, femininity or masculinity. Some of the most commonly cited color associations include the following:

- Red is violent and dramatic; in financial circles, it also has negative associations with the red ink of money loss.
- Burgundy is royal and elegant.
- Yellow is vibrant and happy.
- Green and blue are calm and restful.
- Orange is frivolous and youthful.

Research has shown that this concept extends to certain combinations of colors, giving marketers even more flexibility in using color to convey certain marketing messages. Here is just a sample of the implications of different color combinations:

- Red and green connote authority.
- Red and black represent aggression.
- Yellow and blue imply strength and energy.
- Pink and blue suggest softness.
- White and red signify cleanliness.

In our melting pot society, cultural differences can also play a role. For instance, white indicates purity and cleanliness in some cultures, but it is the color of mourning in others. Since every color carries some degree of political, historical or cultural implication in one market or another, many marketers take a cautious approach that will not offend or provoke any segment of the marketplace. As a result, many corporate identification programs take a middle-of-the-road approach that does nothing to create relevant differentiation or competitive advantage.

The Bottom Line

It is far from an exaggeration to say that an individual's perception of an organization or their propensity to purchase a product or service can be greatly influenced by color. Financial services marketers who understand the nuances of color have a real opportunity to gain marketplace ground by effectively using color to resist the usual. By doing so they can create corporate and product/service branding elements, advertising and promotion that will create an important marketplace statement. The resulting recognition and visibility can be extraordinarily rewarding.

19

Did You Get My Message?

Very few financial products and services possess features and benefits that differentiate them in the marketplace. How then do some manage to build market share while others decline? The answer, in many cases, is that the sponsoring companies use powerful messaging to effectively shape target market perceptions. The marketing messages that are able to break through the marketplace clutter and make financial services offerings appealing to the marketplace are those that make an emotional connection with the target market. Well-crafted, market-driven messaging can completely change a product's appeal simply by placing the marketing focus on specific benefits and attributes that are important to the customer.

The process of developing effective messaging consists of two important steps:

- First, marketers must listen to the marketplace by conducting the research needed to understand the needs and wants of their target markets.
- Then, they must craft key positioning statements and value propositions that most convincingly convey the product/service benefits that address those target market preferences.

We have seen far too many financial services organizations who believe that they thoroughly understand their target market, and then proceed to waste precious resources developing marketing campaigns that address the organization's perceptions rather than the true concerns of the marketplace. Successful marketers know that rigorous market research is the key to crafting benefit-driven messaging that has a direct emotional appeal to target markets.

A Consumer Product Case Study

Experienced consumer marketers have become quite adept at honing effective messaging that can completely change a product's appeal by simply focusing on different benefits and attributes. The history of one everyday consumer product category illustrates quite clearly the power of messaging to drive sales.

Although the toothbrush received a U.S. patent in the 1850s, most Americans did not regularly brush their teeth until after World War II. Soldiers overseas were required to brush their teeth as part of their regular daily routine and spread this practice upon their return home. The mass adoption of brushing by the population soon caused marketers to view toothpaste as a significant product category that held the promise of millions of dollars in sales. Colgate, Gleem and Pepsodent soon became the market leaders.

Then came Crest, the first toothpaste formula that contained fluoride and the first to receive (in 1960) an endorsement from the ADA. There was much to be said about fluoride, and Crest said it well. So well, in fact, that Crest maintained a dominant position in this category for the next two decades.

Competitors eventually grew tired of living in Crest's shadow in this lucrative category. They responded by identifying specific consumer needs not directly addressed by fluoride and telling consumers how their products' unique benefits addressed those needs. For example: Sensodyne relieved the pain of sensitive teeth; Topol, the "smoker's toothpaste," removed nicotine stains; Arm & Hammer cleaned with the freshness of baking soda; Rembrandt whitened teeth; Close Up freshened breath; Tom's was all-natural; Listerine controlled plaque and gingivitis; Biotene managed dry mouth; and so on. Soon there was a proliferation of toothpaste varieties—each focused on a different benefit and supported by benefit-driven packaging and promotional messaging. As a result, by the early 1990s, consumer confusion in this category had reached an apex.

It was at this point that Colgate did some extensive marketing research and decided to take a different approach. They introduced *Total*, a new formula that addressed multiple needs. Among other product improvements, *Total* contained the antibacterial ingredient triclosan to fight gingivitis along with gantrez, which allows triclosan to remain active between brushings. The well-orchestrated launch capitalized on consumer confusion, and the messaging focused on how this new product addressed all the significant needs revealed in their research. The product was an instant success. It immediately became the best seller in the category and built a 35 percent market share in only two months.

Everyone knows that product/service messaging must focus on customer benefits. The saga of the Toothpaste Wars, however, demonstrates one of the most important and least understood factors in the development of powerful messaging: the need to determine whether product/service benefits are independent or interdependent. Our experience shows that messaging is most effective when it recognizes and links interdependent benefits. In order to identify interdependent product/service benefits and incorporate them into comprehensive messages, marketers must first conduct focused marketing research and careful analysis. It can often spell the difference between marketplace success and failure.

Do Not Read Beyond This Point

Unfortunately for financial services marketers, it is not enough to simply create strong, differentiated messaging. Success depends on making sure that those messages are read. We believe that there is a significantly underutilized, time-proven concept that can help marketers create interest and readership: the power of *no*. Every one of us grew up with daily reprimands of what not to do, say, eat, touch or want. As a result, *no* has become one of the most powerful words in the

English language. It invariably evokes a natural curiosity to find out what we are being deprived of. Yet this power is seldom harnessed for financial promotion. Perhaps most marketers intuitively feel that people aren't comfortable with a negative approach.

We submit, however, that a properly positioned negative message will get more attention—and readership—than positive statements. Probably the most succinct, poignant and elegant example of negative messaging is the Ten Commandments, nine of which start with "Thou shall not . . ." A fundamental law of messaging is to first get the reader's attention. Therefore, don't minimize the power of *no*!

The Bottom Line

The creation of strong, benefit-driven messaging is more art than science. It involves a series of interrelated decisions: prioritizing customer needs and wants; determining which benefits are interdependent; matching consumer needs with product benefits; and, finally, deciding how to communicate these benefits in a way that will have the greatest market appeal. There is no doubt that messaging—with its ability to shape marketplace perceptions—is a major determinant of a product/service offering's marketplace success.

20
Big Bucks

The high net worth (HNW) segment has long been a preferred niche market for financial services marketers. Countless numbers of firms have expended considerable resources to develop and promote specialized products and services designed specifically for this rarified market segment. Why all this fuss and attention for a very small percentage of the U.S. population? Well, as Willie Sutton said when asked why he robbed banks, "Because that's where the money is." While the HNW segment represents only 0.2 percent of the population, it represents 10 percent of the country's individual net worth.

A Moving Target Market

Every financial services marketer knows that you can build a productive and meaningful relationship with a group of prospects only if you understand their needs, wants, concerns, preferences and priorities. For years, financial services HNW marketing generally assumed that their target market comprised upscale professionals (e.g., doctors, lawyers and senior corporate officers) who lived in upscale zip codes, drove luxury cars, played golf at their country clubs and traveled extensively.

Then along came Thomas Stanley, a professor from the University of Georgia. He spent years conducting interviews with millionaires and, in 1996, published a seminal work entitled *The Millionaire Next Door*. Stanley made an important distinction between the "Income Statement Affluent," who had big incomes, big homes, big debt and little net worth, and the "Balance Sheet Affluent," whose assets greatly exceeded their debt and other credit liabilities. According to Stanley's research, the typical millionaire was a fifty seven-year-old male from a lower- or middle-class family background who worked his way through college, averaged a fifty-six-hour work week, had been working for twenty-nine years, had a median income of $131,000, drove a Ford and never spent $140 for a pair of shoes or $400 for a suit. These individuals didn't flaunt their wealth, but instead concentrated on accumulating it and growing their businesses.

This new reality ran smack in the face of existing perceptions and existing financial services HNW marketing practices. Marketing professionals realized that their traditional HNW marketing approaches had failed to target a large percentage of the affluent market. Stanley's low-profile millionaires didn't appear on traditional affluent lists because they didn't live in the right zip codes or work in marquee professions. In fact, the research showed that they typically ran small businesses that fall below the radar screen of most financial services professionals.

So, how has this knowledge changed financial services HNW marketing in more than a decade? The short answer is "not much." At a loss for how to effectively reach this group, most marketers continue to rely on the traditional and long-standing perceptions of the HNW segment. The resulting marketing and promotional efforts have largely failed to gain traction because they do not reflect the values or concerns of the target market.

The New Face of High Net Worth Marketing

As a result, there remains a significant opportunity for financial services marketers who understand the needs and priorities of the new HNW marketplace and take the time to develop and implement appropriately customized approaches.

The target market: These are savvy business people and value-driven consumers with primarily middle-class sensibilities who continue to work hard to establish financial stability. These individuals work not in high-profile professions, but rather in low-profile occupations. They are, for example, marine engineers, furriers, printers, construction supervisors and heavy equipment suppliers who are not traditionally targeted as HNW prospects.

The approach: These individuals do not generally respond positively to traditional financial services marketing programs, sales approaches and product pitches. Creating strong relationships is essential in marketing to the "haves and have mores." One approach that has proven successful is known as "relationship mining." This approach focuses on the slower, but ultimately much more rewarding, process of cultivating relationships with the low-profile, non-traditional high-income individual who needs and will value professional advice. Successful relationship-mining practitioners take an interest in the prospect's business, accomplishments and family. They build meaningful rapport by finding ways to help the prospects grow their businesses (e.g., referring family, friends and clients to their businesses or introducing them to local, high-quality service providers). Many have also found that networking with high-income prospects and clients is an excellent way to gain additional information, build trust and acquire referrals.

The Bottom Line

The HNW market holds untapped opportunities for those financial services marketers who are ready to take a less-traveled path and abandon long-held misconceptions about the affluent. Such an approach will enable companies to gain significant competitive advantage by focusing innovative marketing and sales initiatives on individuals generally not identified by traditional approaches.

21
Unite and Conquer: Strength in Collaboration

Listen. You can still hear reverberations from the walls that have fallen down in all sectors of the financial services industry. Not that long ago, a very restrictive regulatory environment virtually mandated that financial services organizations be siloed and very functionally organized.

Then the Financial Modernization Act of 1999, also known as the Gramm–Leach–Bliley Act or GLB Act, repealed the Glass–Steagall Act of 1933. Glass–Steagall prohibited a bank from offering investment, commercial banking and insurance services. The GLB Act removed these barriers and opened up competition between banks, securities firms and insurance companies. GLB proponents argued that money flows into investments when the economy is good and into savings vehicles when the economy is bad. Therefore, since the new act would permit customers to deal with the same financial services firm in good times and bad, the firm would be able to do well in all economic environments.

A Changing Financial Services Landscape

The relaxation of stringent industry regulation created a new openness and flexibility that, in turn, led to dramatic changes in the financial services landscape. Mergers and acquisitions within the industry created a number of multi-range organizations that offered comprehensive financial product/service offerings—many of which were well outside of their established core competencies. At the same time, financial services providers faced increased competition, rising costs and an uncertain economic environment. As a result, firms increasingly realized that traditional organizational structures could not adequately support these new, expanded business models. This realization led organizations to explore a variety of new, collaborative arrangements to develop a faster, less capital intensive approach to respond to the marketplace and stay competitive.

Internal collaboration: Some financial services organizations have found that the creation of interdepartmental, cross-functional teams has helped them reinvigorate their firms and substantially increase productivity by fostering a collaborative approach to marketing initiatives, new business acquisition and service. However, firms considering this approach must understand that successful implementation requires a high degree of rigor and organization. Management cannot simply tell employees to change the way they think and work. They must, instead, provide the training and motivation that employees need to learn how to function as a team and operate in a way that benefits not simply their department, product or service, but rather the organization as a whole. An important first step is to align team goals and compensation. Experience shows that a combination of team and individual goals is the best way to encourage teamwork without sacrificing individual motivation and accountability. It is critical not only to set goals that are both reasonable and ambitious, but also to ensure that all participants understand and agree to those goals.

External collaboration: Innovative financial services organizations are also revisiting the idea of outsourcing in their quest to supplement their capabilities and cope with the demands of the new marketplace. Outsourcing relationships take many forms, from relatively simple, short-term vendor relationships to long-term partnership arrangements in which companies outsource strategic, more complex activities.

Some firms transfer commodity back- and middle-office functions to experts who can provide these services more economically. This arrangement enables the firm to focus on higher-value activities such as product development, distribution and client service. Other firms use third parties to provide new products and services—either until they can build or buy the necessary capabilities or as a permanent solution.

As the financial services industry has become increasingly dependent on advanced technology, many firms have chosen to outsource their technology needs to eliminate large, up-front capital outlays and ensure continued maintenance and upgrades. Other firms have also found that outsourcing their marketing functions can provide immediate access to capabilities, expertise and best practices that may be too expensive or time-consuming to develop internally.

Many experts believe that the future of outsourcing will favor partnership arrangements that involve revenue sharing or incentive compensation as companies seek to stretch their capabilities to deliver a diverse range of products and services while maintaining consistency and control.

The Bottom Line

The market disruption of 2008 led to legislative and organizational changes designed to correct industry ills. During the previous period of deregulation, however, the industry experimented with a variety of new tools and business models in its attempts to keep up with environmental changes. Both internal and external collaborations have proven effective in helping organizations develop new capabilities, enter new markets and gain competitive advantage. In each case, the key to a successful collaboration is a strong, cohesive vision, dedicated leadership and a focus on serving the needs of target markets. The management and marketing lessons learned from navigating this period of unprecedented change should provide financial services organizations the guidance needed to create more effective applications to address the opportunities and challenges that lie ahead.

22

A Tale of Two Categories

Long ago and far away a man developed a theory that would change the lives, both business and personal, of anyone who became a disciple of his thinking. That man was Vilfredo Pareto, an Italian economist and sociologist who lived at the turn of the twentieth century. His theories have widespread applicability and can make anyone a better business-person and a better marketer. First, let's discuss his discovery and how its importance came to be recognized.

It's All Relative

Pareto collected data on income and wealth in nineteenth century England. His data showed that a minority of those surveyed possessed the majority of wealth. The norm across his results showed that 20 percent of those surveyed had 80 percent of the wealth. While that was not surprising, what was of interest was that the relationship between the percentages of people that fell into each category remained somewhat constant across different samplings. Intrigued by these findings, Pareto expanded his surveying and found the same predictable pattern repeating itself with data from different time periods and different countries. Whether the relationship was 80/20, 85/15, 75/25, or anything approximating that, there was a proven predictability in the data.

Pareto's extensive surveys showed that, in virtually all circumstances, the minority of causes leads to a majority of results. Pareto, however, shifted his interests to matters of sociology and never pursued the applications of his discovery. Much later, however, his discovery became known as the *Pareto Principle* or the *80/20 Rule*.

The Pareto Principle lay dormant for decades. Then, in 1932, Harvard linguistics professor George Kingsley Zipf published *Selected Studies of the Principle of Relative Frequency in Language*. The book's central concept—later known as Zipf's Law—was that there is a disproportionate distribution of attention to a few versus obscurity for the many. To illustrate, the most popular word in the English language— "the" (followed by "of" in second place and "and" in third)—is used ten times more frequently than the tenth most popular word and 1,000 times more frequently than the 1000th most popular word. Zipf continued to study applications in this area and published *The Principle of Least Effort* in 1949. This work was a rediscovery and amplification of Pareto's work and provided solid documentation that unbalanced patterns tend to occur in an 80/20 relationship almost universally.

On the heels of Zipf's work, Joseph Juran, an engineer by training, combined statistical methods and the 80/20 Rule and, in 1951, published the *Quality Control Handbook*. Juran developed techniques that identified the roughly 20 percent of problems that caused 80 percent of errors and focused on eliminating those errors, creating greater efficiencies and significantly raising quality standards. His approach was characterized as "the separation of the vital few from the trivial many."

After U.S. industry scoffed at Juran's techniques, he offered to apply his quality control techniques to receptive Japanese corporations. The transformation that took place in the quality of Japanese goods eventually proved threatening to U.S. industry. The United States soon welcomed Juran back so that he could work with domestic corporations to apply his techniques. The result was an American quality revolution that was to last for decades.

Applying the Pareto Principle

As managers in various sectors became familiar with the Pareto Principle they found it to be an effective management tool that, in virtually every area of the organization, could help them improve efficiency and production. By first identifying cause-and-effect patterns, they could then focus their attention on those variables that accounted for most of the problems. For example:

- Senior management noted that 20 percent of the organization's business units produced 80 percent of the revenue.
- Customer service managers discovered that 80 percent of customer complaints were about the same 20 percent of products or services.
- Sales managers found that 20 percent of their sales force accounted for 80 percent of production.
- Project managers realized that 20 percent of the work consumed 80 percent of the resources.

Focusing on the few who contribute the most: The Pareto Principle provides a pragmatic perspective for situation management and can produce invaluable insights to support the development of marketing initiatives that benefit an organization. To illustrate, having discovered that 20 percent of customers account for 80 percent of revenues, marketers might logically decide to

- focus special relationship management and cross-sell initiatives on this elite segment of the customer population
- develop and implement marketing strategies to attract new customers who are clones of those who are currently the greatest contributors to corporate profitability.

To implement these efforts, however, marketers must first identify their most profitable customers and conduct the research needed to create a detailed profile that includes applicable demographic data and addresses subjects such as

- how and why they became customers
- what they buy and how often
- what common characteristics they share.

Reducing distribution costs: Upon finding the 20 percent of marketing efforts that produces 80 percent of results, management might wisely decide to adopt a more focused approach to market penetration. For example, having achieved significant market share in a specific market segment, management may determine that increasing market share in that segment would incur significant incremental costs. Guided by the 80/20 rule, they may instead use those same resources to much greater effect in other segments to gain as much penetration as they can achieve with the least effort.

The Bottom Line

The Pareto Principle (the 80/20 Rule) stands as a continual reminder to focus 80 percent of your efforts on the 20 percent of issues that will produce 80 percent of your results. By viewing and analyzing situations from this perspective, management in all areas of an organization can expend resources more efficiently. Considering that the 80/20 Rule is such a simple analytical tool with such extraordinary versatility, it is amazing that it remains so underexploited.

23

How Do You Measure Up?

John Wanamaker, the department store magnate of yesteryear, once said, "Half the money that I spend on advertising is wasted; the trouble is that I don't know which half." While CEOs of today are certainly nowhere near as sanguine about wasting half of their marketing budgets, very little has changed. One of the biggest corporate questions remains: What value do we receive from our marketing expenditures?

Marketing has long been the corporate exception to the rule that "you can't manage what you don't measure." Those outside the marketing function have traditionally viewed marketers as creative—as opposed to business—types that help maintain corporate image and support sales efforts, but produce unquantifiable results. In recent years, corporations have accelerated their efforts to develop approaches that quantify the effectiveness of marketing initiatives.

What to Measure

The first difficult challenge is to determine which marketing activity to measure. Some of today's most promising methodologies simultaneously monitor a number of metrics to obtain a broad perspective on marketing dynamics. Marketing analysts then study the correlation between the effectiveness and interdependence of related initiatives, as well as the patterns of reinforcement between different activities. The result is a *marketing dashboard*, the newest concept in marketing measurement. This valuable tool arrays the most relevant and predictive metrics in a way that will enable marketers and management to rate performance and identify trends. The best marketing dashboards are customized to the organization's industry, strategy, priorities and objectives.

There is certainly no single measure that can accurately quantify the value of financial services marketing activities that involve a number of financial products, services, customers and distribution channels. As a result, one answer for financial services marketers appears to be a customized, fully integrated performance measurement system that enables a company to develop a marketing dashboard that will provide insights that will guide future decision making.

How to Measure

The next challenge is the determination of what technology to use to perform ongoing monitoring, data capture and analysis. The options range from multi-million dollar installations to do-it-yourself applications that utilize software such as Excel and PowerPoint to gain analytical and graphic capabilities. A functional system will facilitate mathematical calculations and create attractive graphics that will aid the analytical process.

How to Use It

The objective of the marketing measurement process is not simply to acquire and analyze data, but rather to use that data to develop new, more effective marketing initiatives. The marketing dashboard can provide both marketing and corporate executives with insights that will inform their decision making concerning products, services, pricing, distribution, target markets, marketing, promotion and more. Informed, innovative decision making is most likely to occur if everyone involved understands and has confidence in both the measurement process and its results.

Experience shows a direct correlation between the degree of corporate-wide buy-in and the ability to systematically improve marketing effectiveness. The extensive, rigorous effort needed to develop an effective marketing dashboard may be lengthy and trying, but it can reap ample rewards. The ongoing analysis of consistent, accurate data can help an organization

- determine where expenditures are most effective
- develop realistic performance benchmarks and hurdle rates
- identify underperforming initiatives and institute timely termination or corrective actions
- recognize the interrelationships between different initiatives
- gain meaningful feedback and intelligence that can have a number of important uses such as measuring the efficacy of new initiatives and providing data to support budget requests and/or marketing expenditures.

While it may be easier to measure and analyze individual metrics than to continually seek to identify the interrelationships between multiple metrics, this simple approach does not provide the data needed to properly assess multiple products and services in the context of today's highly complex marketplace. Instead, new approaches look at all the aspects of the marketing equation in order to engender the insights and understanding that will enable organizations to move forward with marketing initiatives that will provide a systematically increasing return on their marketing investment.

The Bottom Line

If you don't measure success, you invite failure. While this is true in every area of business, marketing has long managed to get by without providing substantiating metrics to justify expenditures. The tide is now turning for marketers. Technological advances can now support the development of tools and techniques that monitor, capture and organize a wide array of marketing metric data. But effective marketing measurement—like marketing itself—is an ongoing process that is both an art and a science. Technology and number crunching alone cannot reliably identify the strengths and weaknesses of marketing strategies and their execution. Instinct and intuition are critical to determine what to measure, what the numbers mean and what marketing initiatives are called for. It is estimated that less than 3 percent of financial services marketing functions have even undertaken the initial steps toward building a marketing dashboard. This area is still in its formative stage of development, but it promises to be a significant future trend that may ultimately prove the corporate worth of the marketing discipline.

IV
PROMOTION

24
The Secret of Successful Advertising

Many academics writing about the marketing discipline make a distinction between *image* ads focused on creating visibility and goodwill and *informational* (or "reason why") ads designed to motivate readers to buy a product or service. This school of thought contradicts two major principles of our advertising philosophy:

- *All ads are image ads.* The objective of every ad is to enhance the company's marketplace recognition and credibility through the consistent use of visual and verbal brand elements such as logo, tagline, color, graphics and key marketing messages.
- *Advertising doesn't sell products and services—people do.* Advertising's main role is to connect with prospects, shape their perceptions of a company, product or service, and motivate them to take the next step toward becoming a client.

Tips for Developing Effective Advertising

We have, over time, developed a few guidelines that can help facilitate the development of effective advertising.

Tip #1: Focus on the objective of moving the prospect to the next step. The objective could be as simple as motivating the reader to send for an informational brochure, log-on to the company's web site or visit their booth at an upcoming convention. Effective advertising should always help precondition prospects so that sales calls or convention activities meet less sales resistance.

Tip #2: Don't ignore the existing customer base. Advertising can be extremely effective in helping a company reinforce the loyalty of their customers. Advertising effectiveness testing by one automaker revealed that almost 70 percent of those who thoroughly read their ads were individuals who had recently purchased their product and wanted to validate that decision.

Tip #3: Don't indulge in creative concepts at the expense of brand clarity. In today's information age, consumers are constantly bombarded with advertising from a wide range of media. In an effort to develop advertising that will not get lost in the clutter, many creative people focus on producing innovative advertising that does not connect with the marketplace. The unfortunate result is a recurring corporate tragedy that unfolds as follows: An organization develops an effective communication strategy, provides it to the creative types for advertising execution, and then—poof—sees it disappear, beyond recognition, in a cloud of creativity. What remains is artistic advertising that has no relevance to the brand, the target market or the original objective.

Tip #4: "Productive divergence" balances innovation and brand clarity. Productive advertising sends the right messages and actively contributes to a brand's welfare. A productively divergent format, consistently used, can become the company's advertising signature and part of its brand imagery. In time, readers will develop a feeling of familiarity with the format and the company. Familiarity, derived from the same root as the word "family," connotes something in which people can comfortably place their confidence and trust. Opposing the powerful force of the familiar leads many advertisers to make a big mistake: killing a campaign long before it has lost its effectiveness with the target audience.

Tip #5: Make sure the words and graphics work together. The goal is to provide enough graphic interest to catch the eye and then deliver a succinct and poignant message.

When appropriate, graphics that provide visual irony can be very effective. Color is a key element that, when properly exploited, can make a significant contribution to every ad. But graphics should never lead copy. The entire advertising layout should be created so that one thing is accomplished: The first sentence is read. That should start the reader on a path of increasing interest. Well-designed ads control the way a reader looks at an ad, guiding the eye to the elements to be seen first, second and so on. Many ads are too cluttered, failing to heed the KISS principle.

Songs have rhythm; so does copy. Ad copy should have a melodic flow and be clear, simple and to the point. Since language is the currency of the mind, words become the triggers to emotions and desires. Effective copy recognizes that people buy expectations, not products or services, and offers the promise of something better.

The Bottom Line

The nice thing about advertising is that there really are few firm rules. In fact, many of the exemplars are those ads that break the few rules that do exist. A guiding principle for getting the most from advertising: Evaluate what your advertising is capable of accomplishing for your company and then make it do just that!

25
Us vs. Them

The year was 1930 and Sears ran a daring ad favorably comparing its own line of tires to eight national brands. The ad not only created a stir, but also markedly increased Sears' tire sales. Firestone prepared a counter-offensive ad that created such a controversy about business ethics and good taste that many newspapers, including those in New York and Chicago, refused to run it. The controversy subsided, however, and by 1932 Plymouth was able to run an ad entitled "Look At All Three" that effectively depicted Plymouth's superiority over Chevrolet and Ford. As a result, Plymouth's sales more than doubled over the ensuing six months. Comparative advertising had been born.

Over the years, comparative advertising has repeatedly proven its impact and effectiveness. These tactics have delivered significant gains in market share for such firms as Pepsi (over Coca-Cola), Burger King (over McDonald's), Tylenol (over aspirin), Visa (over American Express), Hewlett-Packard (over IBM) and AT&T (over MCI). Reviewing almost 80 years of comparative advertising experience, it is interesting to reflect on some of the lessons learned from those who have done it well and those who have tripped over their own shoelaces.

Ads That Try Harder

The most successful comparison ads not only positively position the advertiser, but also reposition their competitors in a less favorable light. A classic example is the Avis "We Try Harder" campaign. Avis claimed that their second-place position required them to "try harder" by delivering extraordinary customer service. Not only did the campaign extol Avis, but it also took a solid swipe at Hertz. The implication was that the undeniable industry leader was complacent and, as a result, took their customers for granted. Nice going, Avis!

These ads generated significant customer recognition and marketplace visibility. By the time Hertz responded with its own version of comparative advertising, Avis had enhanced its industry position and gained considerable market share.

As Hertz learned the hard way, a strong and immediate fight-fire-with-fire response is the best defense for victims of comparative advertising. With strong response advertising, responders can hopefully level the playing field by providing convincing clarifications and presenting their products/services in a much more favorable light. Response advertising must, however, be carefully developed and implemented to avoid creating a negative reaction. Defensive, unconvincing or ill-conceived response ads can actually increase the credibility of the original attack ads by calling attention to the comparison and failing to counter the points of concern.

Financial Services Applications

The financial services industry provides some high-visibility examples of comparative advertising, some more successful than others. Vanguard, for example, has effectively used comparative advertising to establish itself as the low-cost provider of mutual fund management services in a highly developed niche market.

Schwab, on the other hand, attempted to differentiate itself from the competition with an advertising campaign that extolled its integrity. Unfortunately, Schwab's reach for the moral high ground was executed with the finesse of a playground bully. The attempt to besmirch its competitors' ethics (by accusing them, for example, of "putting lipstick on the pig" to make a sale) not only created animosity in the industry, but also didn't sit well with many investors.

For all its proven power, comparative advertising is a potentially contentious approach that is best used when an organization

- is new in the marketplace or is simply not in a leadership position
- has a relevant differentiation from the competition—especially the industry leader
- has a superior product or service with value-added customer benefits.

The Bottom Line

The history of comparative advertising shows that the consumer goods sector, with its better honed, more aggressive marketing skills, has been much more adept at using this approach than the financial services sector. To successfully implement this potentially effective approach to gain favorable marketplace visibility, marketers must ensure

- first, that all the required factors are in place
- then, that the idea is effectively and appropriately executed.

In the proper situation, targeted comparative advertising can provide a powerful centerpiece for a financial services organization's marketing campaign.

26
Speak Up

The use of a corporate spokesperson has proven to be a highly effective technique for delivering marketing messages. As a result, many companies employ celebrities to bring their aura and panache to corporate promotion. While this attention-getting ploy can be very effective, there are some drawbacks to consider in choosing a celebrity spokesperson.

- *Cost*. High-profile celebrities, such as Tiger Woods, routinely receive in excess of $1,000,000 for a single sponsorship appearance.
- *Relevance*. Mismatching the celebrity personality with the corporate product or service personality—as frequently happens— can dilute the impact of the message. Cindy Crawford, for instance, might be a very persuasive cosmetics spokesperson, but she would be totally ineffective representing a discount broker.
- *The "Wild Card" Celebrity Factor*. Once a celebrity is associated with an organization, their negative behavior can have a detrimental public relations impact on the corporation. Ask PepsiCo, who discarded a succession of celebrities that included Michael Jackson, Mike Tyson and Madonna. Or recall the impact O.J. had on Hertz. Somehow, there must be a better way.

Celebrities, however, are not the only viable spokespersons. In fact, there are a variety of different approaches that can achieve the same—or even better—results without the attendant costs and perils. Let's explore some of these approaches.

Go to the top. Many corporations have successfully used their leadership to deliver their marketing messages. Individuals such as Colonel Sanders, Frank Perdue and Lee Iacocca serve as examples of how effective principals can be in creating the image while delivering the message. They lend an unparalleled aura of credibility because there can be little doubt of their sincerity and knowledge about the organization and its products. However, even principal spokespeople can present problems. When someone like Martha Stewart takes a wrong turn, the inability to separate the principal from the organization can create a public relations nightmare.

Be creative. An effective alternative to an in-house spokesperson is a spokes–character, an invented personage that is relevant to the organization and its products and services. This approach has some real advantages that can make it even more effective (e.g., it does not carry a celebrity price tag and the made up spokes–character can be endowed with a full range of desirable attributes). Think how memorable Juan Valdez, Mr. Whipple, The Maytag Repairman, Miss Clairol, Uncle Ben, the Hathaway man, Aunt Jemima, Betty Crocker, Chef Boy-ardee, the Fruit of the Loom Guys and the Man from Glad have been.

Get animated. A logical extension of the spokes–character approach is the animated corporate icon, which can be extraordinarily effective in delivering memorable marketing messages. Characters such as the Jolly Green Giant, the Pillsbury Doughboy, Speedy Alka Seltzer, Mr. Clean and the California Raisins exemplify the corporate awareness and recognition that a visually unique icon can provide.

Unleash the beast. In a popular variation of the corporate icon approach, the commercial world borrows the Walt Disney practice of projecting human characteristics onto animals to add interest and entertainment to their messages. A few well-known examples include Charlie the Tuna, Tony the Tiger, Morris the Cat, the Energizer Bunny, Joe Camel, Elsie the Cow and Smokey the Bear.

The fact that virtually everyone is familiar with most of the examples cited above confirms the ability of spokespeople—of every sort—to accomplish their communications mission. Creatively conceived and effectively executed, a corporate spokesperson adds another dimension to an organization's corporate messaging. The result is a higher degree of credibility and reassurance that can take an organization one step further in its quest to effectively deliver its marketing messages.

The Bottom Line

Very few financial services organizations have used a spokesperson to deliver their marketing messages. However, occasionally an example of the successful use of a spokesperson—of one type or another—shines through in the financial services arena. For example, Charles Schwab served as his own corporate spokesman, John Houseman's aura of authority assured everyone that Smith Barney had earned it and, from the world of fauna, AFLAC chose its duck. We can only wonder why this powerful marketing vehicle hasn't been more extensively employed in financial services marketing.

27
Let Your Fingers Do the Walking

In this age of information and advanced communications, commercial phone directories (i.e., "Yellow Pages") have maintained their long-standing importance as a reference source.

The origin of commercial directories can be traced to New Haven, Connecticut. In 1718, that city's Collegiate School recognized Elihu Yale's generous endowment of nine bales of goods, 417 books and a portrait of King George I by changing its name and embarking on a program of expansion. The Yale School soon evolved into a major university and spawned a thriving community. By 1878, New Haven needed a catalogue of its growing resources in order to more easily locate suppliers of products and services. In response, authorities printed and distributed a card containing the names of 50 businesses in seven categories—the world's first classified directory.

The idea spread quickly. Around the turn of the century, a tradesman set out to print a more substantial multi-page directory and wanted to differentiate commercial listings and residential listings. His solution was to print business listings on the excess supply of yellow paper that he had lying around his shop. Directory providers have continued this convention to the present day.

After more than a century of growth and despite the dramatic incursion of the Internet into every aspect of our personal and business lives, the "Yellow Pages" remain an important resource. Virtually every marketing budget provides for the placement of appropriate listings in both printed and electronic directories.

Conventional Listings

Printed directory listings provide some unique benefits. First of all, they are ubiquitous. There are more than 150 million Yellow Page directories in print and they are widely available in homes and businesses. Furthermore, they are durable. Unlike other forms of print advertising, Yellow Page advertising is sold on an annual basis and is consulted year round by people who early in life learned the value of this handy reference tool.

Before advertising in the Yellow Pages, a business must decide the size of the ad and the appropriate placement category. Because of the nature of both the medium and the financial services business, we have not been advocates of placing large Yellow Page ads. Whatever the size of the ad, however, there are a few guidelines for developing an effective directory submission:

- *Be consistent.* Organizations with a number of locations should provide all offices with templates that will establish a brand signature and consistency of message across the organization.
- *Keep it simple.* Include a lot of "yellow space," use an easy-to-read type face and avoid clutter.
- *Never pay to use color.* Extensive research has proven that color ads do not out-pull standard "black on yellow" ads.
- *Attract attention.* Make the ad visually interesting by using a distinctive logo or relevant illustration, when appropriate.
- *Highlight the phone number.* This is the most important piece of information in Yellow Pages advertising. It should be prominent and easy to find.

The New Wave

With the amazing growth of the Internet, it is not surprising that more than 40 million people use Internet Yellow Pages every month. It has also been shown that there is little crossover between print and online directories and that a large percentage of Internet directory searches result in a new business contact. As a result, the Internet Yellow Pages provide an important alternative marketing tool for businesses seeking to extend their marketplace reach. Online directories have their own guidelines concerning the size, content and design of ads. However, unlike printed listings, online ads can be placed at any time and generally appear just days after submission.

Looking to the Future

Cell phone companies are responding to intense competition within the industry by searching for new value-added customer services and new sources of revenue. In 2008, there were over 255 million cell phone subscribers in the United States, roughly 84 percent of the U.S. population. Only 15.8 percent of U.S. households currently have no landline telephone service and now rely exclusively on wireless service, but this number is expected to increase rapidly over the next few years. The wireless-only trend is especially prevalent among single-person households, with nearly 20 percent reporting that they have no landline.

In response to this industry growth, the Cellular Telecommunications and Internet Association, a Washington, DC-based trade group that represents the nation's wireless carriers, has been working with major carriers to create a cell phone reference system. These efforts could lead to the development of a hybrid 411 information service that might include a business directory that contains cell phone listings. While the details have not been developed, it is certain that the service will provide yet another valuable advertising opportunity.

The Bottom Line

It is hard for marketers to get enthused about Yellow Page advertising since it lacks the excitement and panache of other media advertising. Consequently, it seldom receives the attention it deserves in the financial services marketing arena. Very little has been done to maximize this underestimated, yet potentially valuable touchpoint for the financial services marketplace. As a result, Yellow Pages advertising offers opportunities for gaining competitive advantage to those who are paying attention to detail.

28

What It Takes to Be Well Connected

Effective communications and customer service are critical elements for corporate success in any industry. Financial services firms, however, face special challenges. They must address client demands for increased communications and fast, reliable access to information while adhering to strict privacy and security guidelines. Financial organizations must also address the critical need to provide both clients and distribution partners with up-to-date product and educational information.

Reaching Out to Customers

Financial services firms historically have been early adopters of technological advancements that promise to provide a worthwhile return on their investment by streamlining their communications and customer service. As a result, the industry has enjoyed increased productivity, reduced costs and enhanced profitability.

The introduction of Interactive Voice Response (IVR) technology was especially advantageous for the financial services industry. IVR turned the ubiquitous telephone into a sophisticated, yet easy-to-use

117

vehicle for information retrieval and data transmission. It soon became the medium of choice for financial organizations seeking a high quality yet economical way to provide both customers and sales representatives immediate access to an array of information. Today, the financial services industry ranks second (behind only the travel industry) in IVR usage.

For a number of years the communications plans of most financial services organizations have focused on the Internet. They have expended considerable resources and expertise to build online solutions that provide information access and interactive capabilities to customers, representatives and employees. The reach of Internet technology, however, has its limitations. While most people have computer access on a regular basis, even regular users cannot always have a computer readily available. At the same time, the accelerated information dissemination made possible by the electronic revolution has fashioned new expectations for immediate information delivery.

The Next Step

We believe that there is a communications advancement on the horizon that holds considerable potential for the financial services industry. It will provide a significant advancement in communications functionality and allow new applications that will be constrained only by the creativity of the implementer. It will also enable applications that create a convergence between the Internet and the telephone. This new advancement is the Voice Portal. Our experience tells us that the effectiveness and adaptability of the Voice Portal will enable it to play a significant role in the future of financial services communications.

The refinement of interactive voice technology has led to the development of user-friendly Customized Voice Portal applications, which enable technology convergences that will greatly enhance accessibility to information. Users will be able to enter data and requests on their computers and instantaneously receive real-time updates or responses from any phone—anywhere, any time. They will also be able to use the telephone to input information directly to a designated web page. There is no need for special equipment and there are no time or place restrictions for user access.

Just a Few of the Possibilities

There are virtually limitless possibilities for Customized Voice Portal applications that can help financial services organizations expand and improve customer service and communications. They can, for example, connect investors to their investments in a number of ways.

One simplified application allows investors to input their investment portfolio on their computers and then, when computer access is not convenient, use the phone to obtain real-time quotes and valuation information or even place a trade. They can also receive phone alerts at specified price points or, on request, get immediate phone notification of a specific company's news releases, earnings or analyst reports. Such an application would be particularly useful for a brokerage firm seeking to offer increased customer service to the millions of mobile professionals who would otherwise find it difficult to monitor their holdings with real-time information during the trading day.

Another possible application would enable a mutual fund company to create a "voice portal intranet" to provide product information and sales training to their distribution partners. This approach would increase the fund company's visibility and strengthen their relationship with their distribution channels. It also levels the playing field within the distribution companies. Now, even the smallest offices in the most remote locations—those that are rarely, if ever, visited by wholesalers—would have continual access to compliance-approved information that they can listen to while driving to work or an appointment. Such an application would extend the reach of wholesalers, provide fund knowledge and sales techniques, bolster sales force morale and create a relevant competitive advantage for the sponsoring mutual fund company.

The Bottom Line

Creative use of new IVR technology has the potential to significantly and cost-effectively improve communications in brokerage, insurance, mutual fund and banking arenas. Early adopters who effectively leverage their leader's advantage will have the opportunity to enhance customer loyalty, gain incremental business and increase market share.

29
Start Spreading the News

While no one can pinpoint the exact origin of public relations, it has long been a part of civilized human communications. The Roman Empire, Asian dynasties, English monarchies and French regimes all had official historians who presented facts in a way that suited the interests of the prevailing rulers. Many of these altered truths have survived through the years as recorded history.

The Genesis of the Modern PR Industry

The first book devoted entirely to public relations, *Persuasion*, was published in England in 1919 and heralded the dawn of a new profession. In our country, the beginning of formalized public relations can be traced to the World War I Public Information Officers who were trained to deal with the press. Returning to private life, many of these individuals began to advise businesses on how to create and/or improve their public images.

John D. Rockefeller's response to his public image problems provided an early example of the power of this young profession. An extremely unpopular figure due to his vast wealth and reputed miserly business practices, Rockefeller employed Ivy Lee, the most renowned public relations counselor of the day, to help him shape a new image.

Among other things, Lee advised Rockefeller to distribute dimes to the public wherever he appeared. This practice became John D.'s trademark and enabled him not only to evidence his generosity, but also to attract a cheering crowd wherever he went. Mission accomplished.

Like John D., we all project personal brand values through our appearance, style of dress, speech, mannerisms and body language. Representative examples of these silent, but highly expressive messages include the following:

- *Shoes*. Footwear is an integral part of personal PR messaging since both its style and condition can make strong statements to others.
- *Timepiece*. With a great divergence of styles and costs, you can be sure that watches tell more than just the time.
- *Smile*. A pleasant visage is a readily accessible but vastly under-utilized asset. While a smile is always there to be mobilized, most underestimate its use as a persuasive messaging vehicle.

And on and on it goes. Every day, countless messages create an individual's persona by either reinforcing the truth or, as is too often the case, sending signals that are out of sync with that person's true character. Every individual sends a stream of messages that causes others to form judgments about them—most often in the first few minutes of contact.

The Complexities of Modern Corporate PR

In a commercial context, an organization creates public perceptions through a similar, but much more complex, messaging system. The endless range of corporate messaging elements includes the company logo; the color and appearance of corporate materials; the content, design and accessibility of the corporate web presence; the office décor; the appearance of the staff; and virtually every interface with key constituencies. Organizations must carefully manage all aspects of their messages to successfully project their self-perceived corporate reality. As the illustration on the next page demonstrates, there is often no such thing as a single reality. Therefore, the essence of good public relations lies in

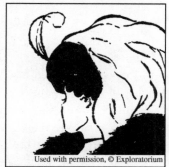

Do you see a young lady
or an old woman?

Used with permission, © Exploratorium

The reality is that you can see
either, or both. Reality truly is in
the eye of the beholder.

- identifying which corporate messages to communicate (i.e., which reality to project)
- delivering those messages in a way that will properly influence each constituency's perceptions, attitudes and behavior.

What makes public relations unique among marketing tools is its ability to announce, explain or validate other marketing initiatives. Strong PR support not only can help raise awareness of other promotional efforts, but can also provide an invaluable third-party imprimatur. Marketing promotions provide a platform for a company to declare, "We are great." Public relations creates a corroborating chorus that informs the public that "They are great."

More and More of the Same

Surprisingly, few financial services firms have found the corporate context to tap the full potential of PR. Most are busy developing press releases that relate daily business activities rather than creating newsworthy stories. In fact, a study of almost 400,000 press releases by Dow Jones Factiva revealed that the twenty most commonly used words and phrases, in order of frequency of usage, were:

1. next generation	8. well-positioned	15. enterprise-class
2. flexible	9. mission-critical	16. user-friendly
3. robust	10. market-leading	17. enterprise-wide
4. world-class	11. industry standard	18. interoperable
5. scalable	12. turnkey	19. extensive
6. easy-to-use	13. groundbreaking	20. breakthrough
7. cutting-edge	14. best-of-breed	

The myriad of hollow press releases that echo one another only add to marketplace clutter.

PR and the Financial Services Industry

Financial services organizations have been slow to adopt sophisticated PR techniques. Many still mistakenly believe that the traditional prolific distribution of press releases constitutes an effective PR approach. We have created our own brand of public relations, referred to as media marketing, to help our clients effectively manage their public relations messaging within the unique dynamics of the financial services marketing environment.

Media marketing is rooted in extensive *planning*, a vastly overused word that describes a mostly underused function in the PR arena. Our approach focuses on achieving strategic objectives by tailoring persuasive interpretations of corporate messages that enable select media to effectively communicate with carefully defined target markets. We understand that the key to receiving the right press coverage and raising visibility in the marketplace is the significance of the issues addressed. Accordingly, media marketing harnesses the technical and intellectual expertise within client organizations to address important financial issues that are of interest to their target media.

The Bottom Line

Public relations generally requires only modest expenditures and can often provide significant rewards. A well planned and effectively orchestrated public relations program can help establish and maintain goodwill and mutual understanding between a financial services organization and its constituencies.

30

Best in Show

The first trade show was the 1851 World's Fair in London, which showcased the achievements of the British Empire in order to generate international business for British companies. This idea first crossed the pond in the form of agricultural fairs that brought buyers and farmers together at harvest time. The success of these fairs soon inspired tradesmen and artisans to conduct similar forums to bring together potential buyers. In this way, the American trade show industry was born.

Today, every industry has trade shows in which outside exhibitors play an important role. Within the financial services industry, conventions—sponsored by organizations such as ABA, ACLI, BSA, FSI, FPA, ICI, LIMRA, MDRT, NAPFA, NAVA and SIFMA—provide exhibitors and attendees with the opportunity to make new contacts, strengthen relationships and learn about new products, services, suppliers, technologies and techniques.

The Phases of Effective Trade Show Participation

For an exhibitor, a trade show can represent either an effective means to simultaneously accomplish a number of different marketing objectives or a significant waste of time and money. The difference lies in careful planning and judicious resource management. Successful trade show participation means much more than simply showing up. To leverage the unique potential that each trade show offers, an exhibitor should launch an intensive marketing campaign that encompasses three distinct phases: pre-show preparation, at-show performance and post-show follow-up.

Pre-show planning: The first step for any exhibitor is to find the shows that will have the greatest appeal for their target markets. Smart companies establish criteria for evaluating a show's potential and, before committing resources, often attend selected shows as observers to gauge the audience and take notes on how to attract attention. The exhibitor should then establish specific objectives for each show (e.g., sales, new leads, product introduction, corporate visibility, public relations and/or product research) based on the audience, the time available and the show's dynamics. All show-related activities should then focus on accomplishing these objectives.

Exhibitors need to be creative if their message is to stand out in a sea of companies simultaneously reaching out to show attendees. A dynamic and creative theme can generate excitement and tie all elements of the event into a memorable experience for participants. To be effective, however, the theme must be reinforced through the booth design, tag lines, promotions, giveaways, communications and all other show elements.

Pre-show marketing can ensure success even before the show begins. Advertisements in the sponsoring association's publication or personal invitations to selected attendees can be very effective if the offer is compelling. People like to be singled out to receive something (e.g., a gift or a free demonstration) that may not be available to the general public.

At-show activities: Three components determine an exhibitor's at-show effectiveness: the booth, the people staffing the booth and the presentation of the firm's products and/or services.

The sole purpose of the booth is to attract attention and encourage attendees to come in. This begins with the sign over the booth, which should *not* broadcast the company's name (as most do), but rather deliver a simple direct message that will attract interest. Words like "new" or "latest" are especially intriguing to attendees eager to learn about industry innovations. The booth itself should be open and non-intimidating, and traffic should be managed through the placement of walls, tables and counters.

Even good salespeople need advance training to effectively manage the unique sales situation found at trade shows. Here, prospects are approaching salespeople (not the other way around), and the number of contacts, the contact time available and the discussion of corporate offerings are quite different from any other sales situation. Unfortunately, most new exhibitors learn by watching other exhibitors. As a result, conformity usually rules, suppressing the creativity and innovation that can create real success.

Passing out product and corporate literature at the show is one of the most common exhibitor mistakes. This only contributes to the trash left outside the exhibition area or in hotel rooms. Exhibitors should instead

- provide an engaging presentation of products and/or services and display available literature
- then ask attendees to surrender their business cards so that they can deliver selected literature to their offices.

Post-show activities: Effective follow-up procedures are essential if exhibitors are to meet their show objectives. A recent survey showed that, on average, companies actively pursue less than half of the leads obtained at trade shows. Before committing more resources to trade shows, companies should measure results against objectives and develop a management report that demonstrates the strategic value of exhibiting.

Resource Management

An effective trade show strategy allocates available resources among the three campaign phases. The truth, however, is that many exhibitors lavish resources on the wrong things. Think of trade shows as having two dimensions: the tangible and the intangible. Tangibles include such factors as exhibition space, exhibit design and construction, shipping and show services. Intangibles include pre- and post-show activities, theme selection, training of booth staff and lead fulfillment. While intangible elements will provide the greatest return on trade show investments, the tangible details invariably receive the lion's share of both resources and corporate attention.

The Bottom Line

Effectively executed trade show marketing provides so many benefits that it can become a meaningful part of almost every marketing mix. The key to being effective is careful planning that will enable a company to take its own distinct course rather than following the exhibitor crowd.

31
Just Cause

Many companies allocate a portion of their marketing budgets to support non-profit organizations. This activity, which has become known as *cause marketing*, provides abundant benefits for both the funding companies and the causes being served. Cause marketing (i.e., "Doing well while doing good") adds a socially responsible component to a company's marketing plan and can enhance brand image and reputation by accelerating corporate awareness within desirable market segments.

Cause marketing is fundamentally about believing in what is good and what is possible. It enables a corporation to make meaningful statements concerning social responsibility, ethics and the public interest. There are hundreds of worthy social issues (e.g., the environment, education, the elderly, diseases, the homeless, children and poverty) that have received much-needed support from cause marketing. In turn, supporting a cause provides the corporation with the opportunity to garner appreciation and recognition from new constituencies who are interested in or loyal to that issue.

A Cautionary Tale

One of the first organizations to practice cause marketing on a national basis was American Express. After reaping considerable public relations benefits from their support of regional causes, they created a highly promoted national program. American Express pledged to make a donation to support the reconstruction of the Statue of Liberty every time a member made a purchase with "the Card." Ultimately, American Express contributed $1.7 million to the Ellis Island Foundation. This ground-breaking cause marketing program was a marketing triumph that provided American Express with a high degree of visibility and favorable recognition.

There was, however, one element of the program that was out of kilter. While social responsibility implies a certain degree of humility that correlates with the perception of a corporation's sincere support for the cause, American Express reportedly spent about $6 million publicizing this program. While their contribution to the cause was undoubtedly generous, critics suggested that it might have been better if American Express had instead provided $6 million to the Foundation and spent only $1.7 million on publicity.

As corporate/non-profit partnerships have become less of a novelty, a new balance between promotion and benevolence has evolved. However, the corporate end-game remains the same: to accomplish a marketing objective while supporting a worthy cause. If properly managed, this is not exploitation but rather a valuable partnership that provides significant mutual benefits.

Tips for Successful Cause Marketing

There are several key components that contribute to the success and relevance of a cause marketing campaign:

Partner: A cause marketing program starts with the selection of the right partner. A safe, non-controversial approach is to partner with a mainstream non-profit organization that has high name recognition and strong public acceptance. The downside of this approach is that it does not provide much marketplace distinction, since many companies provide comparable sponsorships.

Organizations seeking to develop more creative and distinctive approaches should listen to the market to find appropriate cause marketing partners that address underserved public needs. With this approach, however, the stakes are definitely higher, with the potential for significantly higher gains accompanied by greater risk potential.

That, however, is the trade-off that frequently accompanies good marketing programs.

Structure: A partnership agreement should carefully delineate the terms for the creation, management and monitoring of all program components. The parties should agree on a detailed marketing plan that assigns partnership responsibilities and establishes guidelines to orchestrate program activities and the communication of clearly defined messages within each relevant constituency.

Accessibility: As is the case with every good marketing campaign, the success of a cause marketing initiative correlates directly with how quickly and easily people can identify with the message. Therefore, some of the most popular and effective cause marketing events are those that are participatory, visual and media-friendly (e.g., auctions, balls, walk-a-thons, bike-a-thons, golf tournaments, concerts, rodeos, athletic events and art shows).

The Bottom Line

While cause marketing is an accepted marketing tool within the largest organizations, only a modest number of smaller financial services organizations have adopted this powerful marketing approach. Cause marketing provides an excellent opportunity for organizations of every size to generate goodwill while enhancing corporate image and promoting a sense of corporate integrity. Furthermore, in a time when corporate practices and policies are being scrutinized more closely than ever before, it is simply good business to demonstrate that an organization has a social conscience. In addition, working on behalf of a cause can generate support and approval for the corporation from a wide range of constituencies.

Cause marketing, when properly planned and executed, can result in a win/win situation:

- The financial services organization strengthens brand image and loyalty while increasing its marketplace appeal.
- The non-profit organization gains visibility and additional support for its worthy cause.

32

Go Ahead, Judge That Book by Its Cover

Today's financial services organizations face the challenge of differentiating their companies and their offerings in a marketplace cluttered with numerous financial products, voluminous communications and fierce competition. In such an environment, naming a new venture, product or service can be one of an organization's most important marketing decisions.

A name is usually the first connection a prospect has with a company or product. As a result, these few words become the first step in the branding process and bear the burden of making a favorable first impression. Since there are generally only marginal differences between financial product and service categories,

- an outstanding name can make a significant difference in gaining marketplace acceptance and sales
- a bad name can turn away prospects before they learn anything about the product or service.

The Name Game

Here are just some of the approaches that companies use in their search for the right name.

Contrived names: There is a current trend toward using contrived names that not only give no clue to a business's purpose or benefits, but are also hard to pronounce and remember. For example, Verizon combines the Latin word *veritas* (truth) with *horizon*, while Aricent combines *arise* and *ascent*. Lucent means "marked by clarity" and Accenture is derived from "accent on the future." Honestly, most people don't know or care about the esoteric origins of names.

The fact is that any name that does not resonate in the marketplace is a luxury that only a genuinely unique new product or service can afford. Some argue that every contrived name starts out as an empty vessel waiting to be filled with positive perceptions—that, barring any negative connotations attached to the chosen name, the sponsor has total control over what the name means in the marketplace. The counterargument is that it generally requires a substantial (and expensive) branding campaign to generate familiarity and mold marketplace perceptions around a more esoteric name.

Initials: Some firms use initials as their name, hoping to emulate some of the richest and most famous corporations. What these upstarts quickly learn, however, is that the successful use of initials may validate brand recognition, but it does not create it. Companies spend years building visibility and shaping perceptions before leveraging their marketplace success and facilitating brand extension by recasting themselves with their monograms. Think of GE or IBM.

Keeping it personal: A store near our office is called simply Joe's Wine & Liquor Store. This admittedly pedestrian moniker tells customers exactly what they can buy there and who to speak with if they have a problem. While Joe probably aspires to own a store the size of the much larger AAA Liquors further down the road, the name of his current business offers much more appeal for customers.

Innovation and creativity:
On the other side of town is a brightly lit, inviting wine and liquor store with ample parking and attractive displays called THIRD BASE—Last Stop Before Home! Now that's a name and a tag line that get attention from passersby. The name's very suggestion undoubtedly contributes to revenues. This example also illustrates a naming strategy that has long been a favorite of our firm. A brand

> **Tagline: Brand Reinforcement**
>
> A short, engaging tagline underscores a good name by
> - proclaiming the company's customer benefits and/or key brand attributes
> - creating brand awareness more cost-effectively than an advertising campaign
> - helping people make a fast judgment about the firm and its culture
> - embodying the company the way clothes embody the wearer—revealing a lot about the corporate character and brand identity.

name that is appropriately nontraditional for its industry, product or service category will stand out in the marketplace and reduce the cost of building awareness. Distinctive names can be helpful in gaining visibility, recognition and new business because they are more likely to be remembered. Further, a distinctive name creates the perception of a distinctive product or service, while an ordinary name implies that you're just another competitor. It's important to be distinctive—and sound it!

Namer Beware

Naming a new product, however, presents a variety of traps. Many firms add the corporate name or an existing product line name to gain quicker market acceptance. Our experience suggests that borrowing whole or half names almost always creates unnecessary baggage. New products and services are handicapped from inception if they don't have the benefit of a name that reinforces their positioning and helps alter prospects' perceptions of competitive products. A new product or service deserves its own name—one that will immediately go to work for it and it alone.

Politicians are very canny about leveraging the power of a good name. Legislators routinely give their bills names such as "Fair Trade Act" or the "Clean Air Bill" to minimize opposition. Special interest groups like Right to Life or Mothers Against Drunk Driving use their names to rally support. An organization that creates a name that doesn't actively work to differentiate the firm or its offerings might find itself expending substantial resources to gain marketplace recognition. For example, consider the millions AFLAC has invested to gain visibility by turning an educated duck into a media celebrity.

The Bottom Line

The naming process provides an excellent opportunity to put the power of marketing to work for your products and services. It is the important first step in building perceptions that can be continually reinforced by cohesive and consistent messages. The right name serves as the springboard for the implementation of an effective branding strategy. The better the name the more potential it offers for effective, lower-cost branding that can help achieve marketplace success.

V

EFFECTIVE SALES SUPPORT

33

Experience Counts

When I was a child there were times when I would return home past my designated curfew and receive a stern scolding. "But Mom," I would protest, "I was so involved that I just couldn't leave!" Indeed, involvement is a natural phenomenon that has the ability to drive behavior—and not only in children.

Tapping into the power of individual involvement is at the center of an innovative marketing approach that has proven successful for many organizations. *Interactive marketing* involves the customer or prospect in a structured and creative experience that provides a strong identification with the brand. While advertising, direct mail and other forms of marketing promotion can certainly communicate effectively with prospects and customers, the communications flow only in one direction. Interactive marketing enables a firm to listen, as well as be heard. It facilitates a dialogue that focuses on building relationships, rather than on simply describing product features and benefits.

With a customized interactive experience, a firm can create a distinct marketplace presence. It can stand apart from the competition and speak clearly and directly to its customers and prospects—a much better position than fighting for attention as part of a commoditized crowd. An interactive approach can also help a firm build solid relationships with individuals who might never be influenced by sales messages but are won over through the confidence and trust that result from involvement with the firm.

Interactive Success Stories

Several brands, some of which are discussed here, have discovered that involving the customer in a strong and supportive interactive environment can help the firm achieve

- enhanced marketplace visibility and credibility
- stronger, more positive brand identity
- improved client relationships, loyalty and retention rates
- significant incremental revenues.

Both the Nordstrom Experience and the Lexus Experience, characterized by personal attention and extremely flexible service policies, have enabled these companies to stand out and prosper in two very different, yet highly competitive market sectors.

The Disneyland and Disney World empires here and abroad engage entire families in an interactive experience built on fantasy and adventure. Las Vegas, on the other hand, has built an entire city that enables visitors to indulge themselves in a variety of fantastic interactive experiences. They can visit Paris, Rio, or New York, New York at their eponymous casinos or see the sights of Venice at the Venetian. They can live like emperors at Caesars or the Imperial Palace or experience the thrills of Circus Circus. The list goes on and on, with new attractions opening on a regular basis. As they vie for visitors' patronage—and their shopping, dining and gambling money—each hotel and casino pulls out all the stops to provide visitors with the ultimate interactive experience.

FedEx Office (formerly FedEx Kinko's) has opened thousands of locations nationwide to offer an interactive experience customized for the 40 million Americans who work from home. These office centers provide access to printing, computer services, meeting rooms, mailing/shipping and teleconferencing services for entrepreneurs, telecommuters and freelancers who have come to rely on their comprehensive and very accessible office support.

The Financial Experience

With all these examples of how successful interactive marketing can be, one wonders why financial services organizations don't aggressively employ interactive approaches to build more effective prospect and customer relationships. In fact, many financial organizations have made modest forays into the interactive scene with activities such as seminars, financial planning sessions, appreciation events and open houses of various sorts that build interaction into the process.

The few financial services firms that have concentrated their marketing resources on interactive experiences have been quite successful. For example, one high net worth wealth management firm (requiring a minimum investment of $2 million per client) offers to throw a birthday party for each client at a swank local restaurant. The client simply has to name the date and invite twelve friends. The client's account manager attends the party but makes no attempt to solicit business. Instead, the client voluntarily brags that their wealth manager is throwing the party for them, and the guests wonder why they don't get this kind of attention and consideration from their financial advisor. Reportedly, each party produces, on average, one new client for the firm at a very low cost-of-acquisition for this very competitive market segment. The firm largely attributes its meteoric growth to the success of this very personalized interactive marketing/ client appreciation program.

The Bottom Line

By creating a customized interactive marketing experience that is meaningful for prospects and customers, a firm separates itself from marketplace clutter and the need to fight for attention in a commoditized marketplace. The dual goal of any interactive marketing program is to both showcase the capabilities of a firm and involve the target markets that the firm looks to serve. It is important, however, to avoid the pitfall of getting so involved in the experiential components of the program that the marketing message becomes obscured or even lost entirely. The key to developing a successful interactive experience is to use creative approaches and focus on marketing to individual prospects and customers rather than to the marketplace. Today's advance technology can be especially helpful in creating interactive communications and lifestyle marketing that are both compelling and meaningful.

34
Going Up

Remember Professor Harold Hill, the Music Man, who convinced the good people of River City that they needed a marching band complete with seventy-six trombones? Professor Hill was a powerful persuader. He not only created an uplifting vision in the minds of the townspeople, but also persuaded them to make that vision a reality. As a result, motivated parents ordered instruments and uniforms for the many soon-to-become-talented River City children.

What a great lesson for marketers and sales folks trying to make a compelling case for their company's products and services. No matter how complex the organization, anyone can become as successful as Professor Hill with the right tools and preparation. The first step is an effective corporate story, one that enables sales representatives to accomplish the following crucial steps in the sales process:

- *Get the prospects' attention.* To break through the clutter, the corporate story needs to be descriptive and memorable, as well as simple, clear and credible.
- *Tell a convincing story.* An effective corporate story persuasively articulates an organization's value propositions and explains what makes the company different—and so much better—than the competition.
- *Make an emotional connection.* A compelling corporate story paints a vivid picture that enables prospects to envision and identify with the benefits offered.

- *Gain commitment and close the sale.* It is important that prospects take the next step while they are still enthused and motivated.

Take It to the Top

Wouldn't it be nice if everyone in your organization could be as persuasive as Professor Hill? Impossible, you might say. Only sales-people are hired for their ability to communicate and convince, and not all of them are as compelling as Professor Hill. Therefore, wouldn't it be foolhardy to assume that even the most articulate receptionist, accountant or IT specialist could make a solid case about your company's value proposition? Well, yes and no. With a little planning and creative marketing, you can prepare your entire organization to effectively represent your company and provide unconventional sales support.

As the old adage tells us, "You only have one opportunity to make a first impression, so use it well." The best way to make sure that everyone in an organization is ready to make the most of every op-portunity to effectively represent the company is to arm them with a great elevator speech.

Legend has it that the term *elevator speech* began in Hollywood where a writer or director had only the time of an elevator ride in a very short building to pitch a movie idea. The term was later adopted by entrepreneurs who felt they often had a similarly short period of time to make their case to a venture capitalist. Today the elevator speech is an important sales tool used by everyone from job hunters to the representatives of global mega-corporations.

The concept is simple: Assume that you get on an elevator on the ground floor and find yourself standing next to an important prospect. Could you, in the time it takes to get to the fifth floor, be able to convey what your firm does, the benefits it offers and why that pros-pect should be doing business with your firm? If the answer is yes, then you have a great elevator speech.

Experienced salespeople have learned that the value of an effective elevator speech goes well beyond an elevator ride. They always have a well-rehearsed elevator speech ready to be used whenever—and wherever—the occasion warrants.

There is an opportunity for marketers to step in and repurpose the elevator speech from a more creative perspective. The result could be an unconventional form of sales support that involves the entire organization. First, create an elevator speech that is concise and persuasive. Then, make sure that everyone in the organization knows it and understands it. Dissemination is the key to success, so be creative. Laminate the elevator speech on wallet cards for every employee. Embed it in Lucite cubes for everyone's desk. Reproduce it on posters in the lunch room. Encourage managers to discuss the importance of the corporate message embodied in the elevator speech during group meetings. In short, implant it in the hearts and minds of everyone in the organization.

As a result, an entire organization of newly minted salespeople will be prepared when asked what they do and where they work. Whether in a professional or social setting, they will be able to provide an informative, persuasive response that will make a positive first impression. Who knows where that might lead?

The Bottom Line

Marketing's role is to communicate an organization's value proposition and support and facilitate the sales process. An innovative way to accomplish this goal is to use the proven concept of a short and sweet elevator speech to create a program that will prepare all employees to extol corporate virtues effectively and persuasively in all types of situations. While this is both logical and intuitive, it is a mission that few marketing functions assume.

35
Mobilizing an Effective Salesforce

Marketing is more art than science and, as such, provides marketers a lot of latitude in what they can do. In all cases, however, what's important is to focus resources on those things that will effectively support the sales process and help create greater corporate success.

Traditional marketing approaches are, well, obvious. Many non-traditional approaches have been tried and discarded for good reason. There are, however, some innovative approaches that failed to win popularity simply because they were either too new or too complex for successful implementation. One of these too-complicated approaches warrants another look.

Because people know that every form of corporate marketing is biased, they are naturally reluctant to readily accept corporate marketing messages. It is well documented that product claims achieve a higher level of credibility when they are delivered not as pitches, but rather as endorsements from trusted corporate spokespeople. Celebrity endorsements have proven an effective—although extremely costly—approach for companies of all types. The challenge, therefore, is to find a better, readily accessible and much more cost-effective way to secure that same kind of endorsement credibility.

We believe satisfied clients can provide a powerful third-party endorsement for a financial services organization. The key to launching this potent sales force is a focused referral program. With proper schooling and incentives, satisfied clients can positively influence prospects and produce significant incremental business. However, implementing a truly effective referral program can be a complex and rather involved process.

What Makes a Successful Referral Program

The ability to influence decision making: The goal of a referral program is to accelerate a prospect's decision-making process. Research has proven that the product with the better decision support system—rather than the better product—very often enjoys the competitive advantage. When prospects have the necessary information, they can shorten the sales cycle by making decisions more rapidly and with more confidence.

Therefore, the first step in the development of an effective referral program is focused market research to gain understanding of the decision-making process. The goal of the research initiative is to

- map the series of critical steps in the decision cycle that motivates a prospect to choose a financial product or service
- identify the targeted market's values and priorities
- determine the messages and brand attributes that will appeal to the target market.

Tools and materials that motivate the referral network: It is important to equip endorsers with material—whether based on word of mouth and/or word of mouse—that is designed specifically to facilitate communications with their colleagues. Successful programs provide easy-to-use referral tools that

- provide the information prospects need to make an informed decision

- leverage the relationship between referrers and prospects
- enable referrers to transfer to prospects a feeling of their positive experiences with the firm.

Finding the right voice: Successful marketing initiatives adapt their messages to reflect the unique characteristics of the chosen communications vehicle. To illustrate:

- Salespeople interactively provide their most compelling case to convince and close their prospects.
- Advertising focuses on reaching a large number of prospects and communicating important benefits.
- Public relations emphasizes the most newsworthy aspects that will attract the attention of the target audience.
- A referral program needs a story to make its messaging effective.

The development of an effective referral story begins with an analysis of the decision-making research. Where do prospects generally encounter obstacles in the decision-making process? What arguments will successfully overcome marketplace objections?

The resulting story must contain compelling claims, credible promises and benefits that resonate with the target markets. It must also engage endorsers and be short, interesting, convincing and easy to communicate. Above all, since—as with every other aspect of good marketing—success follows truth, an effective story must appropriately manage expectations.

The Bottom Line

A well-structured referral program can help an organization cut through marketplace clutter and accelerate prospects' decision making. By turning satisfied clients into endorsers, a company can create a genuine salesforce beyond a size ever imagined. Given the proper time and attention, a referral program can not only deliver spectacular results, but can also become a responsible and lasting means of increasing sales.

VI
SUPPORTING STRATEGIC DECISION MAKING

36
Slice and Dice

Historically, many financial services powerhouses (e.g., Fidelity, Citi-Bank, Merrill Lynch, MetLife) elected to position themselves as leaders in virtually all segments of the market. As a result, their marketing focused on casting a very wide net in order to attract the largest possible market.

The practices of these industry Goliaths encouraged many financial services Davids to follow their marketing example. Unfortunately, these "me too" marketers did not have the resources to effectively mimic the practices and techniques used by the industry giants.

Trying to pursue every marketplace opportunity is almost always a futile approach and a waste of valuable resources. A more pragmatic, cost-effective approach is one that maximizes the impact of limited marketing resources by concentrating marketing efforts on the most receptive market segments.

Divide and Conquer

The keystone of any successful target marketing program is careful market segmentation based on focused research that provides insights into meaningful customer traits and practices. Segmentation is a process that seeks to partition the marketplace into clearly defined segments (i.e., customer/prospect groupings that have similar characteristics and are likely to exhibit similar behavior).

Segmentation is a key component of strategic marketing planning since it can help organizations to more effectively

- prioritize possible markets and approaches
- identify underserved niches
- capitalize on approaches that achieve competitive advantage.

An effective market segmentation strategy can also significantly help increase sales and improve overall market performance. Its many rewards include new customers, more customers from desired segments, more satisfied customers with products and services that respond to their needs, identification of potentially profitable market opportunities, incremental sales and improved market share.

An Historical Perspective

General Motors provides an early example of successful segmentation. In the early 1920s GM created a differentiated business model by segmenting car buyers into price/quality brackets and then focusing products, messages and promotions to meet the specific needs of each class of buyers. This was the genesis of the renowned family of GM products—Chevrolet, Pontiac, Oldsmobile, Buick and Cadillac. Ford, which offered its standardized Model T in "any color as long as it's black," was caught flat-footed and was forced to close its main River Rouge plant for nearly a year while it retooled in an attempt to regain a competitive stance.

As the GM example illustrates, a firm need not alter its products or services to implement an effective segmentation strategy. It must instead

- effectively match products and services to the identified needs and wants of customers within specified target market segment(s)
- craft focused messages that clearly and convincingly articulate the value proposition offered by these products/services and address the specific needs of the target market segment(s).

Finding Differentiated Approaches

Market segmentation is definitely more art than science. Some of the more common segmentation screens utilize geographic, demographic, socioeconomic, psychographic, usage and/or benefit considerations.

At the same time, however, a number of creative approaches have proven quite effective in analyzing segments. Researchers are utilizing newly refined segmentation to make the process more accurate. As a result, it can often produce uncanny revelations, as illustrated by the accompanying chart.

Regardless of the analytical approach used, however, the objective is to identify market segments that are

- *Unique.* Distinguishable from all other market segments.
- *Substantial.* Big enough to make marketing efforts cost effective.
- *Meaningful.* An appropriate fit with an organization's strategy and resources.
- *Accessible.* So it can be identified and penetrated by an organization's marketing and sales activities.

Top U.S. markets (per capita) for select product categories	
City	**Product**
Atlanta	Aspirin
Dallas	Popcorn
Denver	Vitamins
Grand Rapids	Rat Poison
Indianapolis	Shoe Polish
Miami	Prune Juice
New York	Laundry Soap
New Orleans	Ketchup
Oklahoma City	Motor Oil Additives
Philadelphia	Iced Tea
Pittsburgh	Coffee
Portland, OR	Dry Cat Food
Salt Lake City	Candy Bars
Savannah	Meat Tenderizer
Seattle	Toothbrushes
Source: *Fortune* Magazine	

In looking at the markets for financial services products, we also find that the inclusion of attitude differentiation factors can be particularly relevant. By using appropriate screens as part of a systematic segmentation process, marketers can significantly increase the effectiveness of their marketing messages.

- First, sub-segment prospects/clients based on their purchase dispositions, defined as
  - Innovators: Those who seek out innovation.
  - Early Adapters: Those comfortable with the new and/or different.
  - Mainstream: Those who "go with the flow."
  - Late Adapters: Those that need an extra nudge to "get with it."

- Then, craft specific messages that appeal to prevailing attitudes within each of these groups based on both the disposition of the individuals and the market cycle stage of the particular product or service.

The Bottom Line

While most financial services organizations acknowledge the importance of market segmentation, very few use this powerful tool to its full potential. Too many firms base their segmentation strategies on cursory or intuitive analysis of their markets, rather than deliberate research. We strongly believe that every financial services organization should take a hard look at how to maximize the significant benefits that segmentation can offer.

37

Turning Market Information into Marketing Insights

Over the past decade, increased competition and regulatory change have had a profound impact on the way financial products and services are sold. The challenge has been to progress from product-driven marketing to customer-needs-driven strategies that focus on individual relationships.

A concept as old as marketing itself states, *Don't find customers that are right for your products—find products that are right for your customers*. While marketing literature abounds with the directive to "understand your customer," there is a significant gap between theory and successful practice. A firm can become truly market driven only by listening carefully to customers and becoming thoroughly attuned to their needs.

The Power of Information

Information has played a crucial role in the shift to more focused, customer-needs-oriented marketing strategies. Financial services providers, by the very nature of their business, collect and store a tremendous amount of information about their customers. The longer the relationship, the greater the probability that the customer's transaction history will provide valuable insights about product preferences and the motivation that triggers financial decisions.

Putting Technology to Work

In an effort to achieve industry leadership, forward-thinking financial services providers have employed powerful database technology to incorporate more focused marketing strategies into their marketing mix. We have been impressed by the rate at which database marketing has progressed over the past few years—and somewhat puzzled by the limited evidence of its strategic application in the marketplace.

Today's database technology is capable of providing answers to questions that could scarcely be contemplated even a few years ago. It offers the potential to gain both important micro-insights into crucial customer decision-making factors and a macro-perspective on the current competitive landscape.

The following addresses how database applications can help meet a variety of representative marketing challenges.

Eighty percent of your business comes from 20 percent of your customers. Database techniques can help financial services firms target marketing resources where they can generate the best returns. Database analysis can identify significant patterns and characteristics that are common among a company's first-tier customers. Using this information, the company can then effectively clone those best customers by focusing its marketing expenditures on target markets that exhibit similar behaviors.

You only have one opportunity to make a first impression. Database techniques can help financial services firms optimize the asset-gathering potential of a new product and achieve sufficient initial sales momentum to quickly recover start-up costs. Database analysis enables a company to identify the most receptive market segments for a given product or service. The firm can then create a marketing campaign focused on the needs, wants and preferences of those individuals.

Meet needs rather than push product. When market acceptance is disappointing, it is important to determine if the cause is the product itself or merely the company's failure to effectively communicate the product's most appealing benefits to its most receptive market segments. Database techniques enable a firm to uncover the underlying reasons for the market's response to a slow-selling product. Management can then determine whether a revamped product or realigned marketing strategy would adequately improve sales.

Cross-selling forges multiple links to reinforce client relationships. Research shows that client retention rates correlate directly to the number of products the client uses. The average retention rate is 14 percent for clients who use just one of a firm's products or services, 56 percent for those who use two products and 83 percent for those using three products from the same firm. Therefore, a firm can cement client relationships and enhance account profitability by developing focused cross-sell programs targeting vulnerable single-product households.

It costs five times more to sell a prospect than to sell a customer. One of the most fundamental business maxims is a cardinal rule in financial services: *Nobody does business with strangers*. Converting a stranger to a valued customer requires a significant investment of marketing resources. Database marketing can facilitate the development and launch of effective client retention programs that build stronger customer ties and protect a firm's marketing investment. In addition, since increasing customer retention by 2 percent has the same impact as cutting costs by 10 percent, such a program can significantly increase profitability.

The Bottom Line

Database marketing is a revolutionary marketing tool that can answer important questions and provide a clearer understanding of the competitive forces that drive the financial services marketplace. Database capabilities cannot, however, replace the qualitative elements that are essential to the development and execution of effective marketing strategies. Expert decision making requires a well-developed strategic framework that enables management to

- apply intuitive and creative know-how to the insights provided by database analysis
- develop marketing initiatives that cost-effectively produce increased market penetration and profitability
- achieve a meaningful payback for your database investment.

38

I Know Where You're Coming From

Financial services marketing professionals are constantly seeking ways to identify and refine appropriate target market segments for their offerings. Their ongoing goal is to narrow the focus of product/service marketing efforts to the most receptive groups in order to reduce costs and increase positive response rates.

Database marketing has played an important role in systemizing the segmentation process and introducing a higher degree of science to the art of marketing. Database marketing may not, however, be applicable or available in all cases. There is another highly effective segmentation approach that can help marketers focus marketing resources where they will achieve greater returns, with or without database support.

Birds of a Feather

Early in the last century, social scientists created the concept of *cohorts* or groups of people born in a particular period of time and bound together by shared experiences and historical events. The premise is that people shaped by a particular series of influences share a common value system. As a result, members of different generations react very differently to the same stimulus.

Influences that shape generational perspectives and behavior can arise from many elements or events (e.g., cultural, economic, technological or political). Every generation has comparable rites of passage as they pass through a given life cycle. However, the events that distinguish those formative experiences change from generation to generation and create the basis for a set of associations and responses that help shape common generational values. The chart below cites a number of formative year influences for major generational groups.

Examples of Generational Influences				
Category	Seniors (born before 1943)	Baby Boomers (born 1943–1960)	Gen-X (born 1961–1981)	Gen-Y (born 1982–1997)
Event	Civil Rights	Vietnam	9/11	Global Warming
Fast Food	Automat	Drive-In	McDonald's	Red Bull/ Power Bars
In Touch	Mail	Phone	E-mail	IM/Text
Sports	Babe Ruth	Muhammad Ali	Michael Jordan	Tiger Woods
Night Talk	Jack Parr	Johnny Carson	Dave or Jay	Stewart/Colbert
Media	Radio	Network TV	Cable TV	Internet
Music	Sinatra	Beatles/Elvis	Madonna	American Idol
Comedy	Bob Hope	Lucy	Seinfeld	Adam Sandler
Crime	Capone	Manson	McVeigh	Columbine
Dow	200	800	1,000	10,000
For Kids	Howdy Doody	Sesame Street	Mr. Rogers	Barney
Movies	Gone With the Wind	Godfather	Animal House	High School Musical
Fads	Pogo Stick	Hula Hoop	Cabbage Patch	Pokémon
TV	Ed Sullivan	M*A*S*H	Dallas	Reality TV
Glamour	Betty Grable	Marilyn Monroe	Farrah Fawcett	Paris Hilton
Heart Throbs	Clark Gable	Paul Newman	George Clooney	Justin Timberlake
Hosts	Arthur Godfrey	Dick Clark	Oprah	Ryan Seacrest

While financial marketers should consider the compelling generational orientation of their target markets when refining messaging and value propositions, they should also be aware of the potential pitfalls. The most common mistake is an over-reliance on demographic profiling, a process that ignores the strong values of generational cohorts. For example, many demographic studies assume that people entering a certain age group will display the same preferences and behaviors as those who preceded them. Savvy marketers, however, recognize that even though the priorities of Baby Boomers will change as they reach their sixties, they will not mimic the behavior of the last generation of retirees.

Smart financial marketers also realize that they have their own particular generational perspectives that must be put aside if they are to make sound decisions regarding marketing strategies or product/service development for another generational cohort. While it is extremely difficult for marketers to remove personal values from these types of judgments, it is critical if they are to develop effective marketing initiatives. It often means the difference between connecting with the target market and misjudging it entirely.

The Bottom Line

Good marketing is about satisfying the needs and wants of target markets. Generational cohorts can provide marketers with unique insights concerning the biases, priorities and preferences of market segments. The resulting information can inform the decision-making process and help marketers develop targeted campaigns that will resonate with their target markets.

39

Getting the Right Marketing Answers

For managers in financial services organizations, making decisions that can have a significant corporate impact is part of the job. However, being placed in a position of having to make those decisions without sufficient, reliable information concerning possible alternatives is a major management problem. An effective research support system can provide the competitive and marketplace intelligence that provides a solid foundation for sound and informed management decision making.

The Value of a Marketplace Perspective

"Research is seeing what everyone else has seen and thinking what nobody else has thought." These words from the Nobel Prize-winning biochemist Albert Szent-Gyorgyi wisely convey both the importance and the proper role of research in any creative process. The ability to see things from the point of view of "everyone else" is especially important to those charged with strategic marketing planning and implementation. A financial services organization must first understand marketplace perceptions, priorities and preferences in order to identify (or create) the marketing and brand elements that will help it create relevant marketplace differentiation for the firm and its products. Marketing research can also provide valuable insights in areas such as product development, messaging, distribution channel effectiveness and campaign tracking.

Marketing research is also a valuable tool in ensuring that an organization remains market driven—the mantra of a flood of management books over the last decade or two. Experience shows that failure to stay attuned to the marketplace can cause financial services firms to

- ignore important market shifts or fail to realize when a market has peaked
- abandon core customers and focus on a tempting new niche market
- launch products but have no target in sight
- miss valuable marketing opportunities and fail to successfully reach targeted segments.

What's the Point?

The primary goal of financial marketing research is to help companies ensure that the right distribution channels deliver the right products to the right markets using the right messaging. The keys to a successful research initiative are a specific goal and a focused plan of action.

There are a host of valid research techniques and approaches. As the old adage goes, "There are many roads to the top of the mountain, but when you get there the view is all the same." As a result, it is generally wise to examine alternative approaches before undertaking extensive research. The goal is to work *smarter* rather than *harder*, to select the marketing research approach that provides the right answers in a timely and cost-effective fashion.

Over the years we have developed a variety of pragmatic research techniques that inform and support management decision making.

Here are a couple of examples:

- A company that needs to gauge the potential for a new product would generally launch an extended research project involving interviews and focus groups. However, a company using pragmatic research would begin the quest by studying the historical successes and failures of similar competitive products to unearth some very strong and immediate clues concerning the product's possible fate. As Lord Byron said, "The best prophet of the future is the past."
- A company looking for the best area for a new branch would traditionally expend research resources for site selection studies. With pragmatic research, the company would first look to the sites already chosen by the competition. The fact that a Burger King appears around the corner from most successful McDonald's locations suggests that Burger King has used pragmatic research to minimize the costs of their site selection research activities.

The Bottom Line

Research—like so much else in life—is a good thing that is often used irresponsibly. Responsible marketers understand that a properly conceived and executed research initiative can provide the insights needed to develop new, relevant and differentiated marketing solutions. They use marketing research to support—rather than to substitute for—focused decision making.

Less confident marketers tend to hide behind the data, using reams of statistics to lend credibility to their conclusions. These are the ones who repeatedly declare, "The research shows . . . " and then trot out an array of statistics and charts. Responsible marketers, on the other hand, understand that no research is precise and those who use this imprecise art as a hammer, rather than as a management guide, are both missing its benefits and putting their organizations at a disadvantage.

40

Giving Them What They Want

According to a basic marketing tenet, "If you give people what they need, you can make a living, but if you give people what they want, you can make a fortune!" Focused, in-depth market research is the best way to determine what excites customers and how to get their attention and their business.

In today's highly competitive, oversaturated financial services environment, marketing professionals increasingly recognize the valuable contribution that research can make. While virtually everyone begins a serious marketing initiative with some form of research activity, the degree of skill employed and the amount of relevant intelligence unearthed can vary dramatically.

Marketplace Intelligence = Marketing Power

Focused research is the critical first step in the quest to develop—and successfully promote—market-driven products and services. Its value to an organization goes far beyond the ability to gather accurate facts and information.

The accumulated insights and intelligence derived from systematically collected and carefully analyzed research information can help an organization

- develop customer-focused products and services
- create focused marketing and distribution strategies
- craft a targeted positioning strategy that will create relevant differentiation and competitive advantage within a well-defined market niche
- ensure that the right distribution channels deliver the right products and services to the right target markets using the right messaging.

Good research enables a company to look at products and services from a customer's point of view and develop realistic market perspectives and relevant insights. Research can reveal not only who will buy a product or service, but also when, where, how and why they will buy it. Armed with this marketplace intelligence, a company can develop marketing messages and promotional approaches that will successfully guide customers through the purchase decision process.

Tell Them You Have What They Want

Every marketer knows that customers are looking for products and services that solve their problems and satisfy their needs and wants. Therefore, the test of an effective marketing message is its ability to make a strong benefit statement. The reality, however, is that most financial services marketing does not focus on the customer. Most companies spend millions of dollars attempting to attract customers with features (e.g., performance, yields, product options, ancillary services, etc.). Very few communicate the single most powerful element that can help them close the sale: a compelling benefit statement that clearly addresses the result that the customer hopes to achieve.

According to an old adage, people don't go to the hardware store to get a ¼-inch drill bit, they go to satisfy their need for a ¼-inch hole. As a result, successful marketers have long sought to compellingly illustrate the benefits of a product, rather than the product itself. For example:

- Don't sell fireplaces; sell the glow of embers and the comfort of heat.
- Don't sell marketing books; sell the ability to improve your business.
- Don't sell cell phones; sell social connectivity.
- Don't sell sky boxes; sell prestige.

The most successful consumer product marketers understand that benefit-driven marketing will resonate with their target markets and sell products. To cite just a few:

- Bayer doesn't sell aspirin; it sells a daily preventative for heart attacks.
- Tic Tac doesn't sell breath mints; it sells social acceptance.
- Calvin Klein doesn't sell perfume; it sells sex.
- Coca-Cola doesn't sell a soft drink; it sells "the pause that refreshes."

Time Well Spent

Conducting a focused, in-depth research initiative and rigorously categorizing and analyzing the accrued data are labor-intense activities. It takes time and patience to find the right answers and properly identify marketplace preferences and priorities. It is important not just to probe, but to probe well. The return on the corporate investment, however, is more than commensurate with the resources expended. Good research provides a strong foundation on which the company can build market-driven products and marketing initiatives that will contribute to the bottom line for years to come. As Abraham Lincoln put it, "If I had but three hours to chop down a tree, I'd spend the first two hours sharpening my ax."

The Bottom Line

Financial services providers that haven't done the requisite marketing homework try to entice customers by highlighting the features of their products and services, rather than the benefits they can provide.

However, those who are customer-driven and have established effective competitive differentiation are missing an invaluable opportunity if they fail to take the logical next step and begin to communicate with customers *on their terms*. In brief, tell them you can give 'em what they want. Your reward will be increased marketplace acceptance and significant incremental returns.

41

Some Trendy Thoughts

The degree of an organization's success can often be traced to the effectiveness of its marketing planning process. Effective planning enables an organization to anticipate trends that will impact the business and make decisions based on an understanding of future circumstances, rather than those of the past or present. Wayne Gretzky understood this well. When asked why he was such a great hockey player, Gretzky said, "I don't go where the puck is, I go where it is going to be." In our era of hyper change, marketplace needs and wants shift at warp speed, and the winning organizations will be those that embrace change and pursue the opportunities it offers.

Looking to the Future

Alvin Toffler was one of the first to understand that success lies in anticipating trends, rather than following them. His groundbreaking 1970 work, *Future Shock*—succeeded by *The Third Wave* (1980) and *Power Shift* (1990)—spawned a generation of futurologists who presented intriguing ideas about future trends and how to deal with them. Another noteworthy futurologist, John Naisbitt, gained comparable recognition with his book *Megatrends* (1982), which identified ten critical trends that would distinguish the burgeoning information society from the prior industrial one. Contemporary futurologists

173

continue to refine and promote their theories. Recent noteworthy publications include *Being Digital* (1995), in which Nicholas Negroponte explores the future of communications; *The Art of the Long View* (1991), in which Peter Schwartz demonstrates how scenario planning can help us discover the shape of unfolding future reality; and *The Tipping Point* (2000), in which Malcolm Gladwell shows how trends break into the mainstream.

These and other futurologists have demonstrated that trend analysis is both an art and a science. They have established the value of dismantling a trend to explore its inferences, importance and applications. These concepts have important implications for the corporate planning process.

Leveraging Emerging Trends

Since the influence of an emerging trend grows as it gathers momentum, the greatest opportunities for competitive advantage occur when a trend is still in its nascent stage. Therefore, futurologists carefully monitor many areas (e.g., economic, geopolitical, technological, business, workplace, consumer, investor and societal) for early indications of emerging trends and their attendant opportunities. Such vigilance and insight can produce ample rewards for those who are able to identify and capitalize on important emerging trends. For example, consider the visionaries who first recognized the implications of the innovations that helped define life in the twenty-first century. At the beginning of this new millennium, the government named the following as the ten most influential inventions and discoveries of modern times:

1. Electricity	6. Automobile
2. Microprocessor	7. Internet
3. Computer	8. TV
4. DNA	9. Refrigeration
5. Telephone	10. Airplane

A careful examination of this list reveals that megatrends (e.g., the age wave, the information revolution, global warming, etc.) do not provide the best opportunities for practical business applications. Instead, smaller-scale trends generally offer more frequent opportunities for the development of breakthrough corporate strategic initiatives.

The challenge in looking for viable small-scale trends is to steer clear of fads. Webster defines a fad as "a practice or interest that is taken up with great enthusiasm for a brief period of time." Fads are short-term trends that are almost impossible to predict because they generally have no underlying logic. Hula hoops, many dot coms, chia pets, assorted financial products and pet rocks are recent examples. The only way to successfully participate in a fad is to follow the accounting principle of FIFO (i.e., Get in early, get out early and don't get stuck).

The Bottom Line

The current dynamic financial services market environment provides organizations of all sizes plentiful opportunities to capitalize on emerging trends. To take advantage of these opportunities, however, an organization must have

- a process that enables it to stay attuned to the marketplace in order to identify emerging trends
- a refined marketing planning process that enables the organization to understand the business implications of these trends and determine how to identify and properly leverage the opportunities that will best serve both their corporate objectives and their target markets
- the leadership, discipline and courage to recognize the opportunities afforded by relevant trends and the ability to change priorities accordingly.

Dynamic change constantly occurs in the financial services industry. As a result, financial services organizations continually confront opportunities to be early participants in new trends. Organizations need to stay attuned to the marketplace to identify and reap the benefits of appropriate opportunities.

42
Check It Out

It originated with land surveyors who made distinctive marks, called benchmarks, on rocks, walls or buildings for use as reference points for their topographical surveys. Today, as adapted for business usage, the term "benchmarking" refers to the baseline used for evaluation and measurement.

The Origins of Corporate Benchmarking

Corporate benchmarking formally started only thirty years ago. In 1979, Canon introduced a midsize copier for less than $10,000. Xerox, who could not even manufacture, let alone retail, a similar machine for that price, initially assumed that Canon was deliberately underpricing to buy market share. Over time, however, as Canon's copier sales continued without a price increase, Xerox engineers determined that Canon's more efficient production methods enabled them to sell profitably at these prices. As a result, Xerox decided to benchmark Canon's processes with the objective of reducing its own costs.

From 1980 to 1985, Xerox adopted Japanese techniques that enabled the company to cut unit production costs by half and reduce inventory costs more than 60 percent. This remarkable turnaround by Xerox launched benchmarking as a popular new management movement in the United States. Intrigued by the idea of generating corporate, organizational and marketing improvement by collecting and adapting the best practices of others, many of the nation's leading corporations soon adopted and refined benchmarking techniques. The Malcolm Baldrige National Quality Award formally acknowledged the power and universal applicability of these techniques when it mandated benchmarking for all award entrants.

While benchmarking had its start in manufacturing and heavy industry, a properly implemented benchmarking program can provide significant benefits to financial services organizations. Benchmarking adherents believe that being good enough is never good enough.

The Benchmarking Process

Benchmarking has two basic elements:

1. evaluation of a company's own processes and procedures to identify strengths and weaknesses
2. identification, analysis and adaptation of the processes and procedures of the most successful companies.

Focusing on marketplace needs: Successful benchmarking studies begin with clear objectives that relate directly to the needs and wants of customers and prospects. Clearly stated goals provide a litmus test for corporate decision making and ensure that the process will lead to the creation of products and services that resonate in the designated target markets.

Internal benchmarking: A company must know its own operations thoroughly if they are to serve as the baseline for future endeavors. Therefore, the next step in the benchmarking process is the systematic examination and evaluation of

- internal processes and procedures within and between business units
- the company's marketing approaches for products and services
- the effectiveness of its distribution channels.

One of the greatest benefits of benchmarking is that, if a company learns nothing else, it has a much greater understanding of how its business operates.

Competitive benchmarking: The process then moves on to the systematic study of competitor and industry best practices. A major virtue of benchmarking is that it keeps organizations attuned to changes and trends in their industry sector. Incremental improvements of, say, 10 percent or 15 percent may be more than acceptable until competitors take a radically new approach. An example of such a competitive onslaught is the creation of the Cash Management Account® (CMA®) by Merrill Lynch. Shortly following the introduction of this creatively packaged product, Merrill Lynch was amassing more demand deposits than any banking institution. The banks, on the other hand, continued to routinely strive for greater efficiencies and incremental improvements, thereby ceding their historical dominance in an area of significant profitability.

Expanding the benchmarking focus: The Merrill Lynch CMA illustrates that the most artful part of the benchmarking process is determining where and how to benchmark beyond the obvious direct competitors. The challenge is to identify firms that will be worthy of the resources required to obtain the needed intelligence. An early story of benchmarking illustrates the value of looking outside your industry or market sector.

Early in the twentieth century, circuses traveled from town to town throughout the United States on schedules that often left very little time between performances. The German General Staff sent several of their finest to America to shadow the circuses. From their observations, they learned much about the complicated logistics of striking tents, packing gear, handling equipment and people, and then efficiently setting up at the next location. Although this benchmarking was not done in a military context, the lessons learned were readily adaptable to the efficient deployment of troops in World War I. This story also makes it clear that success lies in the ability not to simply *adopt* existing practices, but rather to *adapt* those practices to the specific situation at hand.

The Bottom Line

Not surprisingly, relatively few financial services organizations have embraced company-wide benchmarking programs. Benchmarking is still generally associated with its genesis in an industrial setting. However, we believe that an effective benchmarking program can make valuable contributions and trigger ongoing improvements throughout an organization. Benchmarking encourages valuable introspection and institutionalizes a measurement system. It also sensitizes the organization to change and helps it to remain alert to opportunities to make quantum rather than incremental improvements. No financial services organization can afford to miss out on these important benefits.

43

Know Thy Neighbor

When it comes to home and family, keeping up with the Joneses is generally not the best approach. In the financial services arena, however, astute marketers understand that it is essential to keep a close watch on all aspects of their marketplace environment (e.g., competitors' activities, economic and industry trends and regulatory changes). Current knowledge of all relevant areas can provide critical insights that can greatly facilitate pragmatic, market-driven corporate decision making and marketing planning.

An Embarrassment of Riches

In this Age of Information, we live in an information-rich nation that provides access to a seemingly endless supply of news, data and opinions. However, while many have long subscribed to the notion that information is power, they are now realizing that the only thing worse than having too little information is having too much. Just think about how frustrating and counterproductive it is to wade through a mountain of data to find the information needed to effectively inform the decision-making process. At moments like this, nobody believes that this surfeit of information confers too much power!

The underlying mistake many people make is to confuse information with intelligence. Information does not become intelligence

181

until careful analysis has identified its significance to the corporation. Therefore, to attain an intelligence-based perspective and create effective competitive strategies, a company first needs a systematic process to gather and analyze relevant competitive information.

Creating a Meaningful Process

Financial services organizations have access to a vast amount of competitive information. Unfortunately, far too many firms have not yet found a way to effectively apply this wealth of information in ways that can help them plan and execute winning marketing strategies. The challenge is to create and maintain a results-driven corporate process that will facilitate the effective access, processing, analysis and utilization of this data on an ongoing basis. A well-designed Competitive Marketing Intelligence System (CMIS) can help meet this challenge.

An important first step is the appointment of a CMIS director who will have overall responsibility for orchestrating and managing the company's competitive marketing intelligence activities. A critical part of the CMIS director's mission is to mobilize the entire organization in support of the company's competitive intelligence needs by

- educating employees and encouraging them to take an active part in the intelligence-gathering effort
- creating a feedback system that enables employees to quickly and easily input information
- encouraging managers in diverse roles throughout the organization to bring their unique perspectives to the interpretation of the information collected and the development of strategic recommendations.

Gathering Competitive Intelligence

CMIS provides a systemized process for monitoring and gathering competitive information on marketplace offerings, product/service commitment, market share and trends, strategic flexibility, new product development, partnerships and alliances, target markets and best marketing practices. This information can help organizations answer a wide range of competitive questions, including:

- *Who*. Any firm in the same market space that could be considered a competitor.
- *What*. Growth/downsizing; mergers/acquisitions; new products/services.
- *When*. Timetables/target dates for implementation of corporate initiatives.
- *Where*. Geographic positioning—local, regional, national or global activities.
- *Why*. Corporate strategies and plans for major activities such as expansion and alliances.

While primary research can provide valuable input, it can be costly and time-consuming. A vast amount of critical secondary information is available from a wide number of public sources, including:

- *Industry, trade and professional associations*. Financial services organizations can obtain valuable competitive intelligence by actively participating in industry groups and associations and subscribing to their publications; and attending industry conferences and conventions; comparing industry and company data regarding sales, customer characteristics, target markets and distribution channels.
- *Distribution channel information*. Financial services sales representatives can provide a wealth of valuable information if they are effectively integrated into the CMIS process. The biggest challenge is the development of an approach to systematically gather field representatives' insights and enter them into the database. Organizations might consider using their national and regional sales conferences to gather competitive input, either through workgroups monitored by CMIS data gatherers or through written or online surveys. The CMIS director should also encourage representatives—via periodic e-mails or newsletter articles—to notify the head office whenever they encounter an interesting piece of competitive information.
- *Corporate communications*. Marketers can obtain valuable information and insights from a variety of sources including

competitors' advertising, marketing material, web sites, press releases, annual reports, want ads and directory listings. Web sites can be particularly helpful since companies can analyze not just the content, but also elements such as incoming/outgoing links, the keywords that are proving successful and the details of pay-for-click campaigns (e.g., search engine placements and ad phraseology).

- *Filings and reports.* The publicly available filings that listed companies must provide to the SEC contain financial and operational facts that these companies would rather not disclose, particularly on such a timely basis. Analysts' reports on these companies can also provide important insights.
- *Court records.* This often overlooked source can provide very revealing and otherwise unavailable information.
- *Third-party web sites.* A number of corporate information sites, including www.hoover.com, www.sec.gov/edgar (which will provide access to the features and capabilities of the SEC's new IDEA system as they become available) and www.corporateinformation.com deserve monitoring.
- *Third-party data providers.* Organizations can also obtain valuable information from sources such as the U.S. Census Bureau, Nielsen, Competitrack or Dialog.

The Bottom Line

Listening to the marketplace has always been an important component of corporate success. A systematic Competitive Marketing Intelligence System can greatly facilitate the process of gathering, organizing, analyzing and using competitive intelligence. More importantly, however, a well-developed and consistently maintained CMIS process can help an organization

- learn what actions competitors might take, not just what they have already done
- avoid unpleasant surprises by providing timely marketplace information concerning possible threats

- evaluate and more accurately interpret where to find the best marketplace opportunities for competitive advantage and how to pursue them
- create marketing strategies that will more effectively allocate limited resources among multiple opportunities so performance goals are more readily achieved.

44

Focus Groups: Is There a Financial Fit?

Consumer products companies have, over the years, expended considerable time and resources to develop innovative marketing concepts, techniques and approaches. While many of these ideas could, with a bit of creativity and testing, be successfully adapted for financial services application, very few firms have been inclined to do so. There is, however, one major exception. Financial service marketers have co-opted and embraced the use of focus groups to identify the best ways to design, price, package and promote products. Ironically, this is one practice that should have been left in the realm of soap powder and snack cakes.

Focusing on the Consumer

Robert Merton, a prominent social scientist, first used focused group interviews in the 1940s to evaluate audience response to radio programs and analyze the impact of army training and morale films. He later coined the term *focus group* to describe a specific situation in which the interviewer asks group members very specific questions about a topic based on considerable advance research. Today market

187

researchers use focus groups to obtain the information and insights that will help them create effective marketing and communications initiatives that will resonate with their target markets.

It has become a marketing truism that the first step in the development of successful communications and promotional programs that will effectively penetrate the minds and spirits of target market segments is to listen to representative members of those segments. Consumer products companies have long seen focus groups as an effective way to listen to the marketplace in a controlled environment.

The Financial Focus

Financial services marketing, however, differs from retail marketing in many important respects. Most significantly, financial services organizations do not offer tangible products or services. They ask people to turn over often significant portions of their hard-earned wealth and trust that the financial institution will take the actions necessary to help secure their future. As a result, an increasing number of financial services organizations build their marketing campaigns on verbal and visual elements that emphasize knowledge/experience, concern for the client and a long-term focus on responsible stewardship. Therefore, the information and insights necessary to develop effective financial services marketing initiatives are very different from the kind of information collected in consumer product focus groups.

Most people are not only willing, but eager, to engage in a discussion on which car, golf club, cola or sportswear they prefer and why. On the other hand, the majority of these same people are reluctant to discuss personal financial matters in any depth in a public setting. When asked what they want from a financial product or service, focus group participants invariably focus on superficial concepts such as lower prices, improved features or more responsive service, rather than their fundamental, deeply felt needs and concerns. As a result, financial services researchers are rarely able to ferret out the counterintuitive concepts and unexpected ideas that could lead to meaningful innovation. Therefore, focus group input generally results in only marginal changes in existing financial products or services, not the new products and services that can help create relevant marketplace differentiation and competitive advantage.

The bottom line is that if you simply want to know the market's reaction to an ad, direct mail package or TV commercial, focus groups will probably provide the required information. However, if you really want to get to the psychology that motivates financial decisions, you will most likely need a more sensitive, personalized approach.

Getting Personal

Individual, one-on-one interviews offer the best alternative for financial services researchers to gather the insights needed to build successful, cost-effective marketing programs. People are generally willing to provide very candid feedback on topics that are important to them if they believe the interviewer is really interested and will protect their privacy. A responsible interviewer sets the tone of each interview by emphasizing that the participant's input will be used only to prepare a composite report that summarizes all of the relevant interviews—with no quotes or attributions. Most people are delighted with an opportunity to offer their opinion and say their piece. The result is a candor and thoroughness that is rarely, if ever, possible in a group session.

A one-on-one setting also provides the interviewer the flexibility to explore topics and comments that can often provide unexpected and highly meaningful input. Therefore, while the conversations with each individual should be highly focused, they should not be scripted or take the form of an oral questionnaire. A more extemporaneous approach enables the researcher to take advantage of all relevant information and insights that could prove useful in developing innovative products, services and marketing campaigns that will resonate in the marketplace.

The Bottom Line

The primary objective of preliminary market research activity is to create effective products, services and promotional initiatives that attract prospects' attention and positively impact their decision-making process. Given the importance of these activities to an organization's long-term success, it seems rather misguided to rely on the public and often stilted focus group process. Financial services organizations would do well to reevaluate if the time, attention and resources that are devoted to focus group research justify the quality and applicability of the results obtained.

VII

PROMOTION IN
THE INTERNET AGE

45

A Brave New World

Change might be inevitable, but these days that inevitability seems to come at an increasingly rapid pace. The world of financial services marketing, for example, no longer changes in a series of small incremental shifts, but rather seems to completely reinvent itself at alarmingly frequent intervals.

The newest development of consequence for financial services marketing is the Internet. It was less than twenty years ago that the Internet became available as a viable business and personal communications tool. Since then, the rate at which it has established itself is unprecedented. Just consider the following:

- It took 40 years for the radio to have 10 million users.
- It took 15 years for television to have 10 million users.
- It took Netscape three years to get 10 million users.
- It took Hotmail less than one year to get 10 million users.

In short, online technology has impacted virtually every aspect of our lives. As a consequence, we even think in different terms. When I was a child a curser had his mouth washed out with soap. Today a cursor is our guide to finding information, conducting research, developing graphics and much more.

Adapting to Change

A major communications advancement rarely comes along. When it does, it represents a new frontier that requires the development of new conventions and protocols. From a marketing perspective, practitioners must perform extensive testing and experimentation to explore the gamut of possible applications in terms of cost, effectiveness, ease of implementation and much more. By analyzing the results, they can systematically and incrementally improve the effectiveness of the various approaches and techniques. As experience and knowledge accumulates, those early adapters are soon able to identify best practices that will provide the foundation for further progress across a wider industry universe.

In the early days of the Internet, entrepreneurial firms on the cutting edge of technology proudly placed their corporate brochures on their web sites and thought they were hot stuff. Now we see just how naïve these early attempts at Internet marketing really were. The field of Internet marketing has grown in both sophistication and in the number of tools and techniques available.

The World of Online Marketing

The Internet has already proven its ability to support and facilitate a wide range of highly effective marketing and sales support initiatives.

Online marketing applications offer many significant advantages over traditional forms of marketing.

- *Flexibility*. Testing copy and creative is much quicker, easier and more cost effective on the Web as a result of real-time tracking mechanisms and the ability to replace or edit copy and creative virtually at will.
- *Transparency*. Webmasters can actually see what a user does on their sites (e.g., what links they follow and what pages make them stop and take the time to read the copy) so that management can identify those approaches that fulfill their success criteria and provide the best return on their marketing investment.
- *Cost control*. Organizations have complete control over the amount they spend on Internet marketing during any given period.

Financial Services Online Applications

Internet marketing has proven to be ideally suited to helping financial services marketers effectively penetrate an increasingly fragmented marketplace. Online initiatives provide an effective, low-cost way to reach a national audience, enhance visibility and produce a significant ROI.

As a result, the Internet has drastically changed the face of financial services marketing, introducing new communications opportunities and challenges alike. Financial institutions are increasingly tapping into the power and potential of the Internet to cost-effectively communicate with clients and prospects alike. These organizations now use Internet applications not only to promote and sell their products and services, but also to increase their brand recognition, expand product and service usage and improve customer satisfaction and retention.

The Internet has dramatically changed the relationship between many financial services firms and their customers. An increasing number of businesses and individuals use the Web as their primary channel for financial account management services and transactions such as bill paying, banking and stock trading.

The truth is, however, that the Internet is still in its infancy. There is little doubt that the best practices of today will be eclipsed by more sophisticated techniques and approaches in a relatively short time frame. The current generation will witness the evolution of the Internet just as an earlier generation witnessed the evolution of television as a communications and marketing tool. Time alone will prove just how much impact the Internet will have as it establishes itself as history's most influential communications and marketing tool.

The Bottom Line

We are in the midst of a major and continually evolving communications revolution. The Internet has profoundly changed the way people communicate, get information and do business. As the field of Internet marketing continues to grow and change, marketers must gain the knowledge and experience that will enable them to evaluate what the Internet can do—both for and to their marketing programs. Marketers need to attune their thinking and become strongly committed to the Internet for reasons of both philosophy and necessity.

46

Searching for the Answer? Maybe the Answer Is Search

It is easy to forget that the Internet has had a very short history. It all began in 1968, when the Department of Defense (DOD) initiated a project to develop a reliable computer networking system. By 1972, the project team had built a basic system that was transmitting the first-ever e-mail messages. By 1973, an expanded system was communicating with the ships at sea and, via packet radios, with troops on the ground. In 1974, developers implemented a standard protocol that allowed communications among all networked computers, regardless of their operating system.

Although the project was funded primarily by the military, the supporting information was not classified. The developers, which included universities across the country, posted the software and source codes on the network as *freeware*. The resulting research and development led to the introduction of the World Wide Web at a scientific conference held in Geneva in 1989. Shortly thereafter, the Commercial Internet Exchange (CIX) was established to provide a universal commercial connection point to the Web. The Internet as we know it was born.

Engines of Change

Soon, a significant amount of information began to accumulate on the Internet. In response, two unrelated pairs of doctoral students took two very different approaches in their quest to develop a mathematical structure that would organize this content and, by extension, enable users to retrieve it efficiently. The work of one team led to the introduction of Yahoo! in 1994, while the work of the other team led to the launch of Google in 1998. The stage was now set for a new world of commercial activity on the Internet.

The launch and subsequent refinement of web search engines completely changed how people used the Internet. Now that anyone could quickly find the information they needed, the Internet was much less intimidating and much more user-friendly. Today, search activities comprise more than 80 percent of online transactions, with U.S. users alone conducting 9.5 billion searches each month.

With the vast amount of content available on the Web, virtually any search yields hundreds of pages of results. In fact, a recent search for the phrase "financial services marketing" found 203,000 exact matches. Research has found that very few users look beyond the first few pages of results. In fact, 85 percent of all new web traffic comes from search engines and 81 percent of search-generated traffic comes from the first three pages of results. Therefore, any financial services organization that wants to drive traffic to its web site must take positive steps to ensure that it consistently appears in the first few pages of search results in the major search engines.

Being a Search Optimist

Search Engine Optimization (SEO) comprises an interrelated series of activities that seek to improve a company's organic ranking on major search engine result pages by promoting the site based on its content and purpose. Effective SEO takes into account the dozens of variables that search engines use to compute the *relevance* (or importance) of a given site. These variables include linguistics, site design, usability, amount of content and linking patterns. In addition, the search engine industry and the algorithms it uses are extremely dynamic. Any site that does not meet a search engine's rules and protocols will not appear in that search engine's results pages.

Internet search activity is driven by keywords, the words and short phrases that web users enter to find the information that they need. Keyword selection is a critical step that can have a long-term impact on the success of any organization's online marketing initiatives. Therefore, the optimization process begins with focused research to select keywords that will attract qualified traffic to the site. Keywords should be specific and relevant to the content on the subject page. Words that are too general can appear in searches that have little, if any, relevance to the site.

Search engines periodically crawl sites to determine their relevance based on keyword selection. To determine how a given page should rank in the search engine's databases, the search engine robots, or spiders, read only certain areas of the page and evaluate the page's links. Therefore, each page should be optimized by making special efforts to clearly identify the relevance of the page using coding to focus attention on titles and descriptions, body text and images.

Rising to the Top

Currently, there are three basic search approaches:

- *Organic search* (natural search or free search) is the original form of search ranking. Rankings are based solely on the relevance of the web site to the keyword(s) entered. Marketing can generate higher organic results for selected keywords by using SEO to manipulate web site design, copy and coding. While SEO can drive traffic over a longer period than *paid search*, it is very time and labor intensive.

- *Paid search* (pay-per-click advertising or PPC) guarantees preferred placement to web sites that have purchased the relevant keyword(s). The highly visible "Sponsored Links" areas generally appear on the top of search engine results pages. While PPC is characterized by quick implementation and adaptability, the cost of popular keywords can escalate rapidly. Other forms of paid search (e. g., contextual advertising, banners, etc.) have also proven effective.
- *Paid inclusion* (paid submission) involves paying a search engine to review the web site for possible inclusion into their search index. While paid inclusion increases the odds that the site will enjoy high placement in the organic search results, it does not guarantee high rankings.

The Bottom Line

Today, the Internet is probably the most effective way for a financial services firm to gain national visibility for its products and services. Because few financial services firms have fully leveraged the power of the Internet, this is an excellent time to cost-effectively achieve competitive advantage. Any organization serious about Internet marketing should begin with a systematic SEO program to improve their organic (unpaid) rankings on major search engines.

47

Cashing In on Clicks

As recently as 2000, many financial services organizations were reluctant to use online marketing techniques to reach out to target markets and promote their product and services offerings. Some just mistrusted the idea of doing business online. Others thought that online advertising was fine for selling consumer goods, but certainly not discrete or dignified enough for the promotion of financial products and services. Well, times have certainly changed! The question now is not whether to engage in Internet marketing, but rather which online methods to use and how to use them most effectively.

Today, the most widely used online marketing technique is pay-per-click (PPC) advertising. PPC ads are sold by major search engines and guarantee that the advertiser's listing will receive favorable placement in the search results for specified keywords. PPC keyword advertising has become an important component of every well-rounded Internet marketing campaign.

How PPC Works

The PPC advertiser bids on specific search keywords that relate to its business or service. The amount needed for a successful bid varies widely based on the popularity of the keyword and the number of advertisers bidding. As PPC usage has increased, the cost of top keywords has escalated and bidding wars have been known to break out between competing advertisers. The ads related to these keywords, which are referred to as sponsored ads or sponsored links, receive preferred placement at the top of the applicable search engine results pages. The exact placement of a sponsored link correlates to the amount of the advertiser's keyword bid. The advertiser pays that amount each time a search engine user clicks on the sponsored link. Hence the name pay-per-click.

Developing a Successful PPC Campaign

The following elements help to enhance a PPC campaign's click-through and conversion rates:

Clearly defined conversion objective: The goal of any Internet campaign is conversion (i.e., getting a visitor to visit the site and take some sort of action). In order to design effective PPC campaigns, companies must first decide if they want visitors to sign up for a newsletter, fill out an application or open an account. This objective will serve as the foundation for all other campaign elements and provide a benchmark for measuring the effectiveness of the campaign.

Effective keywords: Keyword selection is a critical first step in the development of a successful PPC campaign. Proper keyword selection can help reduce overall costs and greatly enhance the program's success.

- The process generally begins with competitive keyword research. Marketers can quickly see what keywords have proven successful for like-minded competitors, the bidding ranges for desirable keywords and if there are overlooked keywords available at relatively modest prices.
- It is also useful to take the searchers' perspective and try to determine what keywords they might enter to find a specific product or service. For example, is a person who wants to buy insurance more likely to enter the product, "life insurance," an

action, such as "buy life insurance," or a benefit, such as "low-cost life insurance rates." Thorough keyword research helps ensure that the phrases selected are meaningful to your target audience and can significantly enhance a campaign's cost effectiveness.

Targeted ad copy: Properly targeted PPC ads invariably produce higher conversion rates than those directed at a general audience. The objective is to develop targeted, keyword-rich PPC ads that not only meet the search engines' specific copy guidelines, but also engage interested parties by communicating key product/service benefits and attracting only those who are valid prospects for that product or service. One of the advantages of PPC advertising is its flexibility; it is relatively easy to test and hone advertising copy to incrementally improve results.

Compelling landing pages: The right keywords and exciting ads can bring users to a specified web site, but it is the mission of the *landing page* to persuade them to take further action. Compelling landing pages specifically relate to the paid keyword and PPC ad copy (e.g., a specific product, service or offer) rather than to the company's overall business.

Conversion metrics analysis: In order to reap the full rewards of even the most carefully designed PPC campaign, a company must track and analyze all of its PPC activity and identify the most effective keywords, ad copy and landing pages. The PPC analyst should first identify the keywords that produce the greatest number of click-throughs, eliminate those that aren't cost effective and then analyze prospect activity to determine how to increase conversion rates. For example:

- *Problem.* Visitors immediately leave the site.
  Possible Cause. A landing page that is confusing or does not relate to the keyword or ad copy.
- *Problem.* Conversion rates are low, but visitors spend time exploring the site and downloading information.
  Possible Cause. The PPC advertising copy, while compelling, doesn't attract prospects that are interested in your offerings.

The Bottom Line

PPC advertising has proven more successful at attracting interested prospects than unpaid or organic search engine listings. According to one study, the percentage of web surfers who click on a search engine listing (the click-through rate) of financial industry web sites is four times greater for paid search listings than organic search listings. This success is typically attributed to PPC's highly visible placement, attractive appearance and ability to engage web surfers through targeted advertising copy. Campaigns can be set up very quickly, and it is extremely easy to update and change messaging and test different creative approaches.

Juniper Research estimates that U.S. companies will spend $7 billion on PPC advertising annually by 2010. Wow! That's real money and a sure sign that PPC is an effective approach for marketing promotion.

48

The Domain Name Game

As the number of web sites proliferates, it has become significantly more difficult to acquire the domain name of your choice. Interesting, descriptive or catchy dot-com domain names have become an increasingly valuable commodity. The following are some of the highest recorded prices paid to secure a coveted domain name.

Domain Name	Amount (million)	Domain Name	Amount (million)
Business.com	$7.5	Loans.com	$3.0
AsSeenOnTV.com	$5.0	Dotnology.com	$2.5
Korea.com	$5.0	Tom.com	$2.5
Wine.com	$3.5	Autos.com	$2.2
AltaVista.com	$3.3	Coupons.com	$2.2
eShow.com	$3.0		

While it is true that many of these sales took place during the euphoria of the dot-com explosion, there is still an active and once again growing aftermarket in domain names. A recent search on

GreatDomains.com, a provider who claims to offer "only the finest in generic, memorable and meaningful domain name registrations," reveals the following interesting offerings:

- Patriots can acquire *america.com* for $1,000,000.
- Losers can change their image by acquiring *won.com* for $750,000.
- Inveterate smokers can purchase *smoking.com* for $500,000.
- Adherents of the Atkins diet can pick up *beef.com* by forking over $150,000.
- Sports enthusiasts can win *team.com* for $300,000.
- Bargain-hunters can get *million.com* for only $200,000.
- And we can obtain *consultants.com* for $189,000. Ouch.

Expanding the Name Pool

Strong demand has significantly shrunk the list of good, available .com names and led to the introduction of new domain name extensions. A perfect example of the lengths to which some people in the domain name market will go is the story of the most recognized two letter symbol in the world—TV—and how it became a widely used Internet extension.

As part of the initiative to assign appropriate extensions to various countries around the globe, the United States was granted the extension *.us* and the South Pacific island nation of Tuvalu was granted the extension *.tv*. In 2000, Tuvalu agreed to license the *.tv* domain extension to The .tv Corporation (now owned by domain industry giant VeriSign) for $50 million. While many originally thought that the *.tv* designation would be appropriate only for companies actively involved in the broadcasting industry, the demand for domain names has spawned an active market for *.tv* names among a wide range of organizations, including auction.tv, with a sales tag of $150,000; jewelry.tv, listed at $35,000; and family.tv, on the market for $60,000. A long list of other *.tv* names is also available in the secondary market.

This extraordinary commercial success inspired others to look for ways to exploit their extension assets. An enterprising London Internet

Service Provider (ISP) rallied support for a plan that seeks to fund the reconstruction of Iraq's Internet infrastructure through the public sale of Internet addresses ending in *.iq*—the country-code extension assigned to Iraq. The organization points out that the letters IQ are associated with the term Intelligence Quotient as well as with the country of Iraq. As a result, they declare that the use of the *.iq* extension would convey a "mark of distinction on the Internet" for certain companies and organizations. For example, members of Mensa International could snap up e-mail addresses ending in @high.iq.

If the Name Fits

While the introduction of new extensions has expanded the list of available domain names, it still takes a bit of ingenuity to acquire a name that suits your company, product or service. In a cyber world that includes well over 100 million distinct sites, the introduction of a new Internet extension represents a singular opportunity to secure made-to-order domain names. As a result, there has been a rush to secure the most desirable names immediately following the introduction of new extensions such as *.net, .info, .name, .ws, .nu, .org, .cc, .sr, .biz, .bz, .tv, .us, .de* and *.cn*.

In response to the incessant demand for new domain names and extensions, in 2008 the Internet Corporation for Assigned Names and Numbers (ICANN) approved the first sweeping change in the Internet's 25-year-old address system. In 2009, organizations will be able to bid for the right to use their own, personally created extensions. As a result, new extensions could reflect a location *(.nyc)*, an industry *(.bank)* or a particular organization *(.UBS)*. Although details are not yet worked out, ICANN will charge organizations a substantial fee for the right to use a new customized extension. This dramatic increase in the number and variety of available web addresses marks yet another step in the dynamic evolution of the Internet.

Staking Your Claim

Domain name registration is a simple process. The purchaser can verify the availability of the desired name and then register it in a single online transaction. To help ensure that a new name will not be challenged at some time in the future, many site owners conduct an additional trademark search before purchasing and using a domain name.

It is also important that site owners understand what rights they obtain when they register a domain name. While a person's home may be their castle, a domain may become their battleground. Since trademark laws govern in this area, the resolution of a domain name dispute is closely tied to trademark rights. Therefore, a person or corporation holding the trademark to a given name or phrase can successfully block the usage of the trademark material in a domain name owned by another entity if

- the domain name (without consideration to the Internet extension) is identical to the registered mark
- the trademark registration predates the date of the domain name registration
- the trademark is federally registered
- the owner of the mark sends the domain owner a cease and desist letter alleging trademark infringement or dilution.

The Bottom Line

In today's supply-and-demand world, a domain name that fits a company's brand is a valuable and important corporate asset that should be carefully chosen and protected. For those who first learn about your company online, your URL is as important a brand element as your company name or logo. A relevant, memorable domain name should, if possible,

- be short and easy to spell
- make use of your company's principal keywords
- contain generic words relevant to your company that people are likely to search
- include a word or phrase that is unexpected and, therefore, likely to be remembered.

49

Plug into Directed Marketing

For many years, marketers have used direct mail to effectively develop or enhance their relationships with prospects and/or customers. Now the Internet has spawned a powerful new version of this traditional marketing tool. *Directed marketing* can deliver results more cost-effectively and more quickly than direct mail. This new approach has special appeal for financial services firms that are increasingly looking to replace mass marketing techniques with more meaningful, customer-centric ways to penetrate target markets.

Directed marketing utilizes many tried and true direct mail principles. The key developmental steps are the same: secure a targeted list, write effective copy, make an attractive offer and create a presentation that will command attention. It is in the execution phase, however, that directed marketing departs significantly from traditional direct mail. Successful directed marketing utilizes new techniques that enable marketers to interrelate with an electronically connected world—a world that represents the new marketing frontier.

Directed marketing is much more than direct mail with free stamps. It is a pure form of bottom-up marketing that is the direct antithesis of mass marketing. Directed marketing makes a direct offer—or appeal—that addresses the unique needs, concerns and preferences of a carefully defined target market segment. The 2008 presidential campaign offered one of the most compelling examples of the power and prevalence of directed marketing. At the outset, each candidate hired directed marketing expertise that enabled their campaign to turn the Internet into an ATM that provided a continuous and relatively low-cost source of campaign funding.

Some Tips for Directed Marketing Success

1. *Effective positioning is the key to successful directed marketing.* A prime example is the American Express Card's positioning as a prestigious financial instrument that brings the privileges of membership to a select clientele. In fact, American Express' winning solicitation letter begins, "Frankly, the American Express Card is not for everyone . . . "

2. *Satisfied customers are always the best prospects.* Every marketer knows that frequent communications can play an important role in helping a company develop and maintain strong customer relationships. The Internet has greatly reduced the time and money involved in the creation and delivery of targeted prospect/customer communications. Directed marketing provides a cost-effective way to reassure customers, motivate customer loyalty, increase retention rates, and launch resell, cross-sell and up-sell initiatives to those who have already committed to the organization.

3. *It's not spam if the recipient finds the message compelling.* It takes careful planning, preparation and testing to develop a directed marketing piece that will make the recipient pause and not hit the delete button. To make sure that each target market segment receives messages that are relevant and targeted, marketers must first develop or obtain a database that segments recipients by demographics, behaviors and interests. They can then develop copy that speaks directly to recipients' individual situations, and design offers that present recipients with an attractive value proposition.

4. *Assess the lifetime value of customers and invest accordingly.* Stringent cost/benefit analysis can spell the difference between focused,

enlightened marketing and taking a stab in the dark. Companies that can quantify the acquisition costs of clients in different categories can then allocate their ongoing marketing budget on those market segments that have the greatest potential to provide a meaningful return on their marketing investment.

5. *Rigorous testing conserves resources.* One of the greatest benefits offered by directed marketing is the ability to test an approach before making a significant commitment of resources. The most successful directed marketers continually test every element of the directed marketing campaign (i.e., copy, creative, customer/prospect lists, timing, offers and even pricing) to systematically and incrementally improve response rates.

6. *Keep budgets flexible.* It is important to always have resources available to exploit unexpected opportunities or expand something that is working particularly well. These unanticipated events often offer the best potential for exceptional returns.

7. *Check your list twice—or more.* Proper list selection is the number one determinant of directed marketing success. Direct response lists *always* outperform compiled lists. It is a good idea to acquire multiple lists—names that appear on more than one list are generally the best suspects and should receive special offers. In addition, meaningful list enhancements (e.g., income, age, marital status, etc.) can help focus offers and create greater response.

8. *The offer makes a difference.* Time limit offers out-pull those with no time limit. Offers with a negative option (yes/no) also produce a greater response. A relevant free gift offer will outperform a discount offer.

9. *Engage the audience.* Directed marketing that utilizes interactive techniques is more exciting and customer friendly—and less likely to end up in the trash.

10. *Explore the many possibilities of directed marketing.* Companies have found that multidimensional initiatives that integrate directed marketing with their print, broadcast, direct mail, telemarketing and Internet activities can create synergies that help them achieve ambitious goals. Many companies have also found that directed marketing has the ability to strengthen relationships with a wide range of constituencies. For example, they use proven directed marketing techniques to cost-effectively communicate with employees, alliance partners and suppliers.

The Bottom Line

The ultimate goal of directed marketing activities is to enable a company to develop, over time, a customized virtual marketplace of individuals that respond to certain aspects of its value propositions. To reach this goal, however, a company must be committed to the directed marketing process. The name of the game is trial and error. Not all lists, messages, creatives or offers will be equally successful. Therefore, the mantra for success is "Test, try, analyze, evolve, repeat and persist." Success will come to those who are willing to try new approaches. In this endeavor, innovation often produces the greatest rewards.

VIII
STRATEGIES FOR LONG-TERM SUCCESS

50
Follow Me

Being a marketplace leader is so important that we encourage every client to work to achieve this positioning—even if it requires them to create a new marketplace niche that they can dominate. Leadership offers significant advantages and many attractive rewards.

Examining Market Leaders

The consumer products area offers several examples of brand leadership. Ivory Soap, to cite one well-known brand, was introduced in 1879 and rapidly gained market share to become the market leader in its category. By 1924, Ivory was a mature product at its zenith, and its future brand dominance appeared to be 99.44 percent guaranteed. However, Ivory failed to follow the strategies that appropriately accompany a leadership position, and one product after another overtook it in its category. Today, with competitors offering varieties of shower gels, liquid soaps, antibacterial washes, aromatherapy bars and moisturizing products, Ivory has been reduced to a minor player in its category.

Believing that Ivory was an anomaly and that an established leadership position was easier kept than lost, Suasion Resources researched other market leaders of 1924 to determine if they had suffered the same fate. The chart on the following page shows how twenty leading products of 1924 have fared over the past eighty-five years. It provides irrefutable evidence that most companies who have worked hard to secure their leadership position also understand that it is just as important to take rigorous methods to protect it.

Brand/ Product Leader—1924	Brand/ Product Position—2009	Brand/ Product Leader—1924	Brand/ Product Position—2009
A1 Sauce	#1	Heinz Ketchup	#1
Campbell Soup	#1	Hershey Chocolate	#1
Clorox Bleach	#1	Jello Gelatin	#1
Coca-Cola	#1	Kleenex Tissues	#1
Colgate Toothpaste	#1	Kodak Cameras	#1
Del Monte Canned Fruit	#1	Levi Jeans	#1
Eveready Batteries	#1	Life Saver Candies	#1
Gillette Razorblades	#1	Sherwin-Williams Paint	#1
Gold Medal Flour	#1	Singer Sewing Machines	#1
Hammermill Paper	#1	Wrigley Gum	#1

The Advantages of Market Leadership

A company gains more than bragging rights by becoming and remaining a brand/product leader. It gains the leader's advantage, a term that refers to the many benefits that accrue to a leadership position. Leadership is not an end result, but rather the beginning of a company's opportunity to exploit and leverage these advantages to remain well ahead of the competition.

Advantage #1: A heightened level of marketplace trust. The credibility imparted by market leadership facilitates a company's ability to acquire new businesses and build market share. Loyal customers who place their trust in the company generate repeat business and unsolicited referrals that invariably provide the market leader with positive marketplace visibility and superior customer awareness within their segment. As a result, customer communications and promotional campaigns are better received and, consequently, more effective.

Advantage #2: Economies of scale that result in increased profitability. As sales increase, a company can reduce operating expenses by leveraging its infrastructure and enjoying the resulting economies of scale. As a result, margins improve and returns on investment expand. Market leaders are also in a better bargaining position with their resource suppliers, another factor that helps them improve margins and enhance ROI.

Advantage #3: Greater opportunities for expansion and improvement. Most market leaders invest significant amounts of their surplus in R&D to provide new and higher quality products and services. In addition, leaders are able to enhance their capabilities to maximize productivity by attracting the best management. All this adds up, over time, to greater competitive differentiation and an enduring leadership position.

Adopting a Leadership Strategy

Most financial service marketers recognize that a leadership position can help a company withstand competitive assaults and maximize its marketplace opportunities. At the same time, however, they question if the quest for leadership is appropriate for most financial services organizations. We strongly believe that the answer is yes, but only for companies that are willing to commit to developing and adhering to an aggressive leadership strategy.

This is a key point that cannot be overemphasized: Securing a market leadership position is a *critical strategic planning issue*. A company cannot achieve leadership simply by launching clever advertising campaigns or corporate promotions. Nor can it achieve leadership by becoming the largest spender in its segment.

The Bottom Line

In our commoditized financial services business, product or service successes can be easily replicated. As result, a company's future can depend on management's willingness to invest resources to conceive and implement an effective strategy to achieve market leadership. That decision will place a company in one of two camps: those that forego present earnings for future results or those that will later wish that they had done so.

51
Good, Better, Best!

There is a valuable corporate asset that lies hidden in most organizations—the information, intelligence and expertise resident in their own corporate management teams. Companies that successfully mine this corporate knowledge are often able to create more effective marketing strategies, stronger value propositions, improved processes, increased customer value and innovative product/service offerings. The net result is operational excellence, greater efficiency and enhanced profitability.

While most executives are more than willing to share what they know to help the greater corporate good, many organizations present geographic, structural and/or cultural hurdles that thwart this natural inclination. In such an environment, a carefully constructed, systematic program can help create the focused interaction that enables key decision makers to identify and implement an organization's own best practices.

The Search for Internal Best Practices

An internal best practices program that consciously dismantles organizational barriers to share corporate knowledge can be one of the fastest and most effective ways to achieve organizational improvements. Unlike corporate reengineering and other change efforts, these internal programs enable an organization to tap into the real experiences, knowledge and intelligence of those who have won their stripes dealing with the organization's culture and challenges.

The simple objective of an internal best practices program is to identify the most effective existing practices and determine how to adapt and improve them for implementation throughout the organization. We believe that a deliberate, multistep process can help surface the full range of relevant issues and ensure that they are addressed with the required intensity. Key steps in the development of an internal best practices program include:

- *Participation*. The involvement of key decision makers from various disciplines is critical to the success of an internal best practices program. The first step, therefore, is to assemble a management team that includes representatives from all functional areas.
- *Idea audit*. Initially, the selected management team should brainstorm ideas, issues and approaches to identify those initiatives that have the greatest potential to help the organization meet key objectives.
- *Building consensus*. The management team can then conduct one or more structured workshops that will not only serve as a forum for further exploration of selected ideas and initiatives, but also encourage a team dynamic and create a sense of ownership within the group.
  - During the kick-off meeting, participants address a series of questions and tasks that help them to systematically reach consensus on assumptions and goals for the organization, target markets, growth plans and distribution priorities. They also begin to weigh the viability of various courses of action.
  - At subsequent meetings, participants will explore corporate best practices that can potentially help management maximize the efficiencies of the organization in specific areas. Participants prepare in advance of the session so that they can help the group understand, review and evaluate proposed new processes and procedures.

- *Taking action.* After each workshop, the management team determines the most appropriate next steps based on the issues identified and the degree of consensus reached. For example, a task force could be created to detail the actions and resources required to implement one of the best practices under consideration.

The Bottom Line

An internal best practices program not only can help optimize the efficiency and profitability of corporate changes and improvements, but also can generate valuable understanding, insights and joint commitment among management teams. We have successfully conducted our internal best practices process in organizations large and small, always with rewarding results. The power of the process is truly remarkable. Management teams have walked away with, at the very least, a clearer definition of their objectives and, at best, a thoroughly revitalized sense of purpose and direction.

52
Be Prepared

In recent years, the exposure of corporate improprieties and the accompanying intense media scrutiny has created heightened cynicism and distrust of business among the American public. This environment is especially troublesome for financial service organizations since their success depends in large part on their ability to create marketplace confidence and trust. It is critical, therefore, that every financial services organization always be prepared to respond to a crisis in a way that will preserve credibility.

Most financial services organizations devote a myriad of corporate resources to creating and reinforcing trust through advertising and product/service promotion. At the same time, however, these same companies spend very little corporate effort to create an effective crisis management strategy to protect that hard-won trust. Experience shows that prior preparation can provide substantial corporate rewards since, even in some of the most troublesome circumstances, the real issue often becomes not the incident itself but the way it is managed.

Mayor Rudolph Giuliani's actions during the catastrophic events of 9/11 provide a notable illustration of the positive results of proper crisis management. Time's 2001 Man of the Year proved that preparation, instinct and common sense, coupled with effective communications, can play a major role in handling even the most extreme situations favorably.

What It Takes

Past crises can teach important lessons about how an organization can successfully deal with what could become a devastating incident. Our experience helping clients through a wide range of crises has taught us that the critical aspects of crisis management include the following:

- *Timing*. When a crisis hits, an organization's response should be swift and to the point. It is important that an organization take control and get the bad news out as quickly as possible, rather than give a third party the opportunity to leak the news and use it to their own advantage. A delay in disclosing an adverse situation only invites negative conjectures and hyperbole.
- *Responsiveness*. During a crisis, an organization should avoid providing a "no comment" response to the press or any of the company's various constituencies. In a crisis, people demand quick, incisive information. Companies who evade the hard and important questions cede control of the situation and invite the public to turn to other sources that may have little, if any, interest in protecting the organization or fairly depicting the situation.
- *Access*. The most successful crisis management strategies utilize a multidimensional communications program to quickly and accurately disseminate critical information that will convey the real story to its various constituencies. Good communications also can prevent confusion and embarrassment by providing all constituents with the ability to provide ready, consistent answers to relevant questions. The Internet can prove particularly useful in providing organizations with a way to continually provide updated information to interested parties. Many companies place banners on their home pages to alert visitors to where to find the latest information. Some have even used paid Internet advertising to ensure that individuals using search engines to find information about the event are directed to the company's own site and not that of a third party that is looking to promote its own interests.
- *Candor*. Honesty does count. If the crisis is the result of mistakes or omissions within the organization, management should make candid, straightforward statements concerning the nature of the problem and, most important, how and when it will be corrected.

However, if the organization stands falsely accused, the corporate spokesperson (who under these circumstances should probably be the CEO) should be strong and indignant, providing a full and complete factual rebuttal to dispute the false allegations.

The Bottom Line

A crisis can represent a turning point in a company's history. How the organization responds to that crisis often plays an essential role in determining the future course of that history. The guiding rule for a successful outcome lies in the five Ps: Prior Planning Prevents Poor Performance.

Companies seeking to successfully shape opinion and remain credible in a crisis must effectively manage perceptions while bearing in mind that success will follow truth. It is, therefore, important that every financial services organization have a crisis management plan that guides all parties—management, corporate spokespersons, sales representatives, et al.—on how to handle unexpected events. That ounce of corporate prevention can be worth pounds of attempted cure.

53

An Older Subject

Most mainstream financial services organizations acknowledge the growing financial power of the senior market. Very few, however, have managed to develop effective strategies that leverage that power to benefit both the seniors and their own firms.

By the Numbers

By the time the last baby boomer turns sixty-five, the sixty-five-and-over population will have doubled since the onset of the millennium. In 2000 there were 35 million individuals over the age of sixty-five, representing 12.4 percent of the U.S. population. It is projected that the number of seniors will exceed 40 million by 2010, reach 54.5 million in 2020, and climb to 71.5 million—about 20 percent of the population—by 2030. As the baby boomers enter the senior sector, Americans are also living longer. In 2000 the sixty-five to seventy-four age group was eight times larger than in 1900; the seventy-five to eighty-four age group was 16 times larger; and the eighty-five-plus age group was thirty-four times larger.

These dramatically changing demographics represent extraordinary marketplace opportunities for the introduction of new financial products and services. There is already a growing demand for financial products and services that focus on specific needs. We anticipate that new financial companies will enter the marketplace, further extending the boundaries of the ever-widening financial services landscape. A few firms have already enjoyed a great deal of success with highly specialized products that address the needs of aging Americans. For example:

- The business of some reverse mortgage lenders has increased more than 50 percent annually.
- A relatively new sector in servicing senior needs, the life settlement business, has grown at an average annualized rate of about 20 percent.

Serving the Financial Needs of a New Breed of Retirees

The key to successfully serving this generation of 71.5 million people, who will soon control the lion's share of the wealth in this country, is to recognize that most baby boomers are not interested in pursuing a traditional retirement of leisure. Market research shows that a large segment of this highly educated, goal-oriented generation indicates that the need for continued mental stimulation and challenge—much more than financial concerns—will motivate them to continue to seek various degrees of active employment throughout their retirement years. At the same time, boomers will spend significantly more time in retirement than their ancestors. Today, a 65-year-old stands a better than 50 percent chance of living to at least 85 and a 30 percent chance of reaching 90, according to a MetLife study.

By rejecting traditional retirement, living longer and better, and choosing to work or cycle between work and leisure, baby boomers will reinvent retirement—a fact that has profound implications for how financial practitioners advise this generation of clients. Boomers will extend their earning, saving and investment compounding years far into their retirement. In addition, many will not have to utilize retirement savings as their primary source of income until much later than current planning models indicate.

In fact, many boomers are already rejecting old strategies for meeting their wealth-management needs, recognizing that their needs are strikingly different from those of their parents.

- They want more sophisticated analytical models that employ detailed asset-allocation and financial-planning processes and/or integrate expert opinions on topics such as elder care and budgeting.
- Many will seek "family office" style arrangements that will enable them to confidently outsource the burdens of wealth as they pursue their dynamic lifestyles.

A Slow Start

So far, however, relatively few financial organizations have taken steps to tap into the potential of the senior market in any meaningful way. As a result, financial organizations have made little progress in identifying effective strategies that will help seniors preserve their capital and improve their financial circumstances. Just consider, for example,

- how much literature financial organizations produce about saving for retirement, and how little about investing during retirement
- how many strategies they offer for 401(k) investing, and how few for harvesting that money
- how much guidance they offer concerning dollar cost averaging, and how little concerning systematic withdrawals.

Taking Aim

Any organization that seeks to generate significant revenues from the senior marketplace must be willing to devote the time and resources needed to encourage breakthrough thinking and develop innovative products and services that resonate with the senior psyche. They should begin with meaningful research that will enable them to answer the following questions:

- What are seniors' highest priority financial needs?
- Which of these needs best corresponds to our core capabilities?
- Where can we provide the greatest value?
- Do we need new products/services/divisions to establish ourselves as senior market specialists?

- What is the cost of developing new offerings to meet evident, underserved needs?
- What level of commitment are we willing to make to this market segment?

The most successful companies will be those that devote the ideas, capital and talent required to make seniors a meaningful part of the organization's focus over the long term.

The Bottom Line

Significant future trends rarely signal themselves as overtly as the oncoming senior revolution. There is also no doubt that it will have a profound impact on the nation's economic environment—from saving to spending, from housing to healthcare, and more. What a shame it would be if financial organizations failed to take the steps needed to strategically evaluate the long-term benefits of effectively positioning their products and services within the senior sector.

54

Bringing Order to the Meeting

"Oh no, not another marketing meeting! We must be starting another new project." It's a corporate cry that is becoming increasingly familiar as the marketing meeting phenomenon continues to run rampant in the financial services industry.

The Need to Meet

Financial services organizations today find themselves in an increasingly cluttered, extremely aggressive competitive environment. To gain competitive advantage in this dynamic arena, many companies create task forces to consider a host of possible growth initiatives such as developing new products and services, entering new target markets and exploring new distribution channels. As projects become more encompassing, marketing's success is increasingly dependent upon the ability of knowledgeable representatives from different disciplines across the organization to work together as an effective team.

Unfortunately, corporate tradition continues to dictate that frequent group meetings are the primary vehicle of communication and coordination for task forces, despite the proliferation of readily accessible alternative forms of communications (e.g. e-mails, faxes and PDAs). Therefore, as companies convene more task forces to address a wider number of corporate challenges, the number of group meetings increases exponentially. Many complain, however, that far too many of these meetings are unnecessary and do nothing to help people work together creatively and productively.

A New Kind of Meeting

Some of the most progressive financial services marketing departments are beginning to use an alternative approach that makes much more productive use of time and talent and accomplishes what the meeting marathon should but rarely does. They are abandoning the sometimes unlimited and quite often unproductive traditional meetings in favor of multidisciplinary project team sessions that foster communications, involvement and solid decision making.

Instead of the string of meetings that continually hash over the same problems, these task force pioneers convene topic-centric facilitation sessions that have significantly more potential for quicker and greater productivity. This highly structured process, under the leadership of a trained facilitator, utilizes a specialized style of communication that maximizes group creativity, interaction and commitment. Experienced facilitators have mastered the tools and techniques of successful group facilitation. They systematically help the group to generate, manage, organize and evaluate a wide range of relevant concepts, ideas and data, and then develop strategies that lead to problem solving and solutions. The facilitator's other diverse responsibilities include

- conducting a well-structured, mission-driven meeting
- helping the group build team spirit and group solidarity
- managing conflicts
- ensuring that the group develops conclusions, consensus and cogent next steps.

Experienced facilitators understand the need to create a team environment and instill a feeling of accomplishment early and often during the session. To do so, they

- begin the session by having the entire group agree to the session's mission and goals

- make sure that everyone is involved and contributes as an integral part of the team effort
- employ problem-solving and implementation tools and techniques to help increase group productivity
- set a tone that encourages innovative thinking
- create a forum to identify variance of purpose and provide for amicable conflict resolution.

These market-driven facilitation sessions create a totally new group dynamic. They empower multidisciplinary group project members to work together to plan projects, make decisions, solve problems and guide their own work.

The Bottom Line

Marketing departments should welcome the opportunity to break the cycle of unproductive and prolonged meetings in favor of sessions that focus efforts and get results. Utilizing the effective tools of facilitation, marketers have only to assemble a diverse, multidisciplinary team that will focus on developing solutions for a specific project, and then disband it as soon as it has achieved its objectives. When the next project arises, a new group of multidisciplinary participants with appropriate skill sets are selected and given the challenge of a carefully focused mission. This pragmatic, results-oriented alternative to traditional meetings provides a dynamic approach for increasing the effectiveness of marketing initiatives as well as productivity and organizational effectiveness.

55

And They Lived Happily Ever After

Market conditions have accelerated the merger and acquisition activity that has characterized the financial services industry over the last few years. The industry has experienced not only traditional mergers, but also consolidations that have produced mega-corporations that have significant influence across the industry. As a result, although each sector of the financial services industry consists of numerous small- and medium-sized entrepreneurial firms, the concentration of power is with the largest players.

Consider these statistics:

- Five banks account for more than 60 percent of all credit card lending.
- Ten life insurance companies account for approximately 45 percent of the industry's assets.
- Ten commercial banks control more than 50 percent of the industry's assets.
- Ten mortgage companies control almost 40 percent of the market.

- Ten online brokers are responsible for about 65 percent of online trading volume.

The Two Sides of Every Deal

When a merger or acquisition is contemplated, virtually everyone focuses on the quantitative side of the ledger. Those in charge of M & A activities pore over details such as the multiple of earnings that should be factored into the terms of the deal or the discounted cash flow rate of return for each of the entities.

There is also, however, a less analytic, more qualitative perspective that must be considered if a firm wants to fully realize the potential of a merger or acquisition. Ultimately, the reason for any such transaction is to achieve the benefits that synergy will bring. It's the constant hope that adding one and one will equal three. To make that happen, however, management must implement a focused program to align divergent interests and realize the synergies promised by the deal makers as soon as possible after the closing.

Time Is of the Essence

While companies are bigger after a merger, a question often remains as to how much better they are. This is a question of great relevance to the various stakeholders with an interest in what happens at their financial services organization. Significant commitments of capital, time and talent have already been made by the time a merger or acquisition is consummated. Prolonged disruptions in integrating operations and achieving economies can significantly dilute the time-value of returns to unacceptable levels. Senior management needs quick paybacks to justify the investment and fund continued growth.

Evidence suggests, however, that successfully integrating merged companies is not an easy feat. In fact, there is research suggesting that, following the merger, approximately one-half of merged entities underperform their industry peers. At the same time, however, a merger presents an unprecedented opportunity to shape the future character, direction and profitability of an organization and to focus the firm, its people and its products for sustained long-term growth.

Hurdles to Overcome

Financial institutions within each sector are dissimilar in as many ways as they are similar. While they all operate under the same general rules and regulations, each has its own culture, history, systems, expertise and idiosyncrasies. As a result, merging two organizations is a substantial undertaking that represents as many challenges as it does opportunities. Just as every merger or acquisition is the unique product of its component organizations, it follows that every set of post-merger challenges is unique to the management team that must resolve them.

Further, it is inevitable that individuals involved in a merger will experience some degree of anxiety. Change can lead to instability, and instability can lead to anxiety, which can directly impact productivity and earnings. The challenge for management is to proactively anticipate such distractions and counter them before they negatively impact business.

Getting Off to a Good Start

Proactive strategic direction of the integration process is essential to the timely optimization of the resources, capabilities, image, goodwill and market momentum of the combined entities. Management needs to employ a carefully managed process to derive the potential benefits of acquiring and assimilating complementary businesses. That process should start with an element that is often missing—buy-in from both sides of the merged entity.

A well-structured, senior management offsite can often provide the foundation for building consensus and understanding among parties on both sides of the newly-formed organization. A carefully prepared and professionally facilitated meeting gives participants an open and collaborative forum to

- present new ideas and perspectives
- struggle with hard questions and reflect on issues about which there is often a good bit of uncertainty
- share their experiences and express their judgments, ideas and biases

- scrutinize assumptions and discuss implications
- develop hypotheses and draw conclusions.

The synthesis of different points of view leads to the development of a well thought out integration plan that has buy-in from key management and will prepare the entire organization to respond more rapidly and consistently as the process proceeds.

The Bottom Line

An effective post-merger integration process recognizes the need to capitalize on synergies and reconcile differences *promptly* in order to create a new momentum that enables everyone to move on to maximum productivity. Marketing's applied skill set can prove extremely valuable in orchestrating a post-merger integration process that can make a significant difference to the resulting success. Unfortunately, senior management all too often overlooks marketing's potential contributions amid the frenzy of the deal-making process and the challenges that follow.

56

Putting Humpty Together Again

When the going gets tough and the business appears to be headed due south, the powers-that-be soon demand that management turn things around and right the wrongs. This represents a turning point for any business and the subsequent decisions can have long-term consequences that are often well beyond original expectations. It is imperative that anyone in this situation think carefully about how to approach the needed fixes, as the future of the business is at stake. Companies that respond appropriately to challenges will *survive*. Companies that anticipate change and develop appropriate strategies to manage will *thrive*.

When a business is failing on a transactional basis, management's response will most likely be to find transactional remedies (e.g., slashing budgets that aren't providing current revenue, selling selected assets to raise working capital and reducing the workforce). All too often, the result is an impaired organization that faces the future without the resources needed to compete effectively and grow aggressively.

The Road Less Traveled

There is another course, a radical approach that stands in stark contrast to transactional leadership. *Transformational leadership* seeks to develop and implement long-term solutions that will restore corporate health and then grow the business to new heights.

239

Some high-profile exemplars of a transformational approach include Lee Iacocca at Chrysler, Steve Jobs at Apple, Ferdinand Piech at
Audi and Lou Gerstner at IBM. These leaders faced daunting challenges
and created a new corporate reality that changed the way every
constituency perceived and experienced the organization.

Transformation is about breaking the shackles that keep an organization from realizing its full potential. Big leaps in growth and performance are often constrained not by competition or market forces, but
rather by self-inflicted handicaps. Breaking these bonds requires more
than strategic thinking. It may demand the power of constructive
revolution. By assertively challenging conventional wisdom, a corporation can take a bold and unexpected stance that captivates the
marketplace and creates immediate and relevant competitive advantage.
Visionary leaders intuitively comprehend when maintaining the status
quo may be more dangerous than launching into the unknown.

There are three factors that are essential for effective transformation:

- *Commitment.* Visionary leadership is the catalyst that drives a
  successful corporate transformation. A visionary leader makes
  the commitment to aggressively confront reality at every step of
  the process and to go beyond incremental changes and stop-gap
  measures. Instead, the visionary leader focuses on transforming
  the business and creating something new and more effective.
- *Vision.* Effective transformational leaders understand the need to
  develop and communicate a clear and compelling vision of a
  new and highly desirable future that will permeate the entire
  organization and beyond. A compelling vision will not only
  serve as a beacon for multiple transformational initiatives, but
  also help people release their hold on the status quo and embrace
  new approaches and behaviors. A successful vision is a balancing
  act. It utilizes existing resources and capabilities to the fullest
  extent possible. It also acknowledges what no longer works and
  embraces new possibilities that will support the organization
  throughout its journey to accomplish the vision. It identifies the
  major transformational objectives and lays the groundwork
  for initiatives that will realign the internal functions of the

organization. The vision enables every part of the organization to become mutually reinforcing and supportive of the process.

- *Action.* To implement this transformational vision, leadership must proceed to create a fact-based business success model by consistently and systematically confronting reality, reallocating resources and establishing goals that stretch the organization beyond its current comprehension and capabilities.

The Bottom Line

Financial firms face unprecedented challenges in today's environment. To maintain relevant marketplace differentiation, organizations must adapt not only their products and services, but also their brand image and marketing approaches. The corporate transformation process can help financial services firms redefine and reposition themselves in the marketplace without negatively impacting corporate stability and client confidence. It is a process that maintains great sensitivity to the organization's capabilities, competencies and culture. When appropriate, corporate transformation can provide a highly effective way to create relevant differentiation, secure competitive advantage and attune an organization to current and future market opportunities. In fact, given the inherent benefits, a savvy strategy might be for an organization to consider a corporate transformation before falling into crisis.

57

Counting Dollars and Making Dollars Count

The old adage is that "the exception proves the rule." The rule governing the contents of this book was that each chapter should discuss a specific topic that can impact the success of a financial services marketing program. This chapter is the exception, offering a brief commentary on two important marketing issues.

Is the Price Right?

There is not a chapter on pricing in this book. That is not an oversight but rather a conscious decision. There are numerous books on pricing policies and strategies. These tomes include lengthy discussions and mathematical formulas for approaches, such as cost–plus pricing, which adds a markup to cost; competitive pricing, which sets price relative to the competition; and relationship pricing, which aggregates services with a single price.

To ensure that it properly prices its products and services, a company should adopt the prospect's point of view and remember that *price is only an objection in the absence of perceived value.* Pricing, like all marketing efforts, should recognize the needs and priorities of the marketplace. The right price is the one that makes prospective customers believe that they are receiving benefits that are at least commensurate with the cost.

Organizations that spend an inordinate amount of time and effort trying to arrive at the optimum pricing may be missing the point. They should remember that perception is still the major factor in pricing and concentrate on those factors that target markets will consider in determining whether an offering carries a fair price.

Does Marketing Matter?

For years, up cycles have seen dramatic increases in marketing budgets and down cycles have seen dramatic decreases. Management seems to be declaring that they do not consider marketing a productive business initiative that can make a significant contribution to the bottom line. After all, would any thinking management respond to bad times by cutting back on any activity that they believe stimulates business and provides a meaningful return on investment?

The real question, then, seems to be whether marketing is indeed a wasted expenditure in most financial services organizations. Unfortunately, marketplace evidence shows increasingly mediocre financial marketing campaigns and an ever-diminishing display of best marketing practices. We have witnessed many ill-conceived strategies, as well as an array of tactical marketing programs that in no way articulate the sponsoring organization's strategy.

Prove It!

The onus remains on financial marketers to maintain the credibility of marketing within an organization. They must do everything in their power to measure the effectiveness of marketing efforts—during good times and bad. In this way, they can amass the evidence needed to make a compelling case for continued management support of marketing expenditures, even when budgets are being cut.

Going against the Flow

True believers in the power of marketing will, in concept at least, reserve funds when budgets are plentiful so that they can increase marketing expenditures in down markets. This tactic provides companies with increased marketplace visibility just as competitors are reducing their marketing commitments. They achieve competitive advantage by standing tall in a less-cluttered marketplace.

We have long made the point that the business of financial services organizations is not selling products or services, but rather instilling trust. The down part of every cycle naturally produces a diminution of public confidence. Organizations that send reassuring promotional messages to their target markets during the more difficult times can win loyalty, incremental market share and marketplace respect. These gains are more than temporal. This countercyclical effect perpetuates the marketing cycle of success for organizations that understand financial marketing dynamics and are willing to make the required commitment to create this success.

Those who have championed marketing through a number of cycles will find this an intuitively appealing approach. Yet few financial services marketers have been able to implement an effective countercyclical program. Marketers need to make a strong, cohesive case to overcome the management objections to implementing such a program. They must present marketing campaigns that have expressed, market-driven objectives and incorporate meticulous measurement of their effectiveness. A disciplined approach enables a receptive management to confidently share ownership of the program and appreciate the contribution that marketing can make to corporate goals.

The Bottom Line

Two points to consider:

- First, when financial services marketers price their products or services, they should always remember that price is only an objection in the absence of perceived value. Focused research and well-crafted marketing messages can help a company communicate value propositions that are commensurate with their pricing.

- Second, if you don't measure marketing success you will invite failure. By benchmarking marketing success in good times, marketers can make a case for allocating more marketing resources in down cycles in order to make an impact on the marketplace while competitors have reduced their marketing budgets or retreated entirely.

Afterword
Some Parting Words

I hope that this book has provided you with a number of thoughts, ideas and insights that can help you make your marketing programs more effective.

The intent of this book is to take financial services marketing practitioners out of their comfort zone and motivate them to explore new techniques and approaches. The ideas and concepts presented here are meant to serve as catalysts for innovative thinking. The challenge to the reader is to take ownership of those concepts that have relevance to their situation and adapt them for integration into focused, objective-driven marketing programs. To conclude, I offer a few additional thoughts about achieving financial services marketing success.

Innovate

The marketing process is fueled by innovation. Tomorrow's successes depend upon the ability of individual marketing practitioners to fearlessly follow the path to marketing innovation:

- *Step 1*: Create a vision.
- *Step 2*: Formulate a strategy to realize that vision.
- *Step 3*: Develop an integrated marketing plan that systematically addresses how to implement that strategy with multidimensional

programs that skillfully combine a number of market-driven approaches.

Experiment

Those concerned about the risks and uncertainties of new approaches should remember that the difference between a rut and a grave is its depth. In marketing, the rewards of sensible experimentation far outweigh the risks. One cannot overstate the value of testing to the success of any marketing initiative. It is important, however, to remember the following guidelines:

- Testing is only a tool. The objective of the testing process is to gather sufficient pertinent information to identify and improve what works while abandoning what doesn't.
- Choose variables carefully. The variables tested must be meaningful enough to yield information that will allow a systematic and incremental improvement in results. The definition of insanity is doing the same thing over and over and expecting different results.
- Many times the greatest insights come from the most unexpected places.
- It is imperative to critically assess the variables tracked and the information received to confidently determine if a given approach will repay an expanded investment with the desired results.

Look Inward

Many marketers think that the primary mission of marketing is to attract new customers to their firm. Wrong. Just as important as the acquisition of new customers is the retention of current customers. One of a marketer's primary duties is to convert available customer data to marketing intelligence and use that intelligence to develop programs that will enhance the customer's attachment and loyalty to the company.

Financial services firms have a decided advantage because of the amount of detailed information that they have about customers and their households. Yet, while most financial services organizations are data rich, they are action poor.

If your firm's database is inaccessible for marketing purposes, create your own. Gather valuable data that will provide the insights needed to do some effective customer-centric marketing. For example:

- *Survey your best customers*: Find out why they keep coming back for more. Focus on their buying process and learn, for example, in what order they purchase various products and services. Find out about unmet needs and concerns that your firm could address.
- *Survey your inactive accounts*: Find out why they're not doing business with you now. Find out where they are currently doing business and why.
- *Look at the complaints your company receives*: You will probably uncover a lot of information about customers' priorities and concerns.

By carefully analyzing all the customer data you can access or gather, you will begin to understand not only what each market segment needs, but more importantly, what they want. These insights will give you a solid foundation for some effective customer-centric marketing.

Reach Out to Customers

Interaction with the marketplace is changing rapidly. Since today's technology provides customers and prospects with instant, on-demand access to a wealth of information, companies no longer have the ability to determine what information customers should have—and when. In this environment, little things like small personalized one-on-one marketing approaches can make a big difference in a company's efforts to build customer loyalty that can benefit resell, cross-sell and up-sell efforts. Far too often, however, these little things fall through the cracks of the marketing planning process. Few companies take the time and effort to systematically and consistently address the human side of enterprise.

It takes only a modest amount of thought and attention to cost-effectively strengthen relationships with customers through systematic customer outreach initiatives. A birthday card shows thoughtfulness and caring. An occasional sincere note simply thanking customers for their business can have great meaning. Taking the time to schedule in-person reviews can make a strong personal statement.

Embrace Change

Marketing is dynamic and continually offers new challenges. Marketing success will come to those who read the tea leaves and are able to both anticipate and appropriately respond to both current marketplace realities and emerging trends. Here is just a taste of what is in store for marketers:

- A new marketing model is emerging. It advocates marketing that is inclusive, interactive and responsive. As a result, many traditional marketing elements (e.g. print advertising) will continue to fall out of favor as others (e.g. online marketing) increasingly take their place.
- There are seismic shifts occurring in the marketplace (e.g., the aging of the baby boom generation) that will motivate companies to create new products, services and approaches to aggressively court favor in influential market segments.
- The balance of power among distribution channels is also changing dramatically (e.g. full service brokerage vs. independent contractors) and product/service providers will have to refine their marketing and sales support efforts if they are to realize the greatest channel distribution possibilities.

Get Involved

Marketing is now a participatory sport. In coming decades, successful financial firms will be those that make marketing the responsibility of the entire organization, beginning with senior management. In an industry that is long on management and short on leadership, those who understand the importance of marketing to the success of their organization will gain considerable competitive advantage.

Personally, I cannot imagine a more exciting business field than financial services marketing. It provides infinite and varying challenges that make me spring out of bed each morning anxious to seek solutions for the unresolved questions from the day before. I do hope you feel the same. Happy is the person whose work is play; may financial services marketing provide you with a fertile playground!

About the Author

Jay Nagdeman is president of Suasion Resources, a specialized organization that provides marketing consulting services exclusively to clients in the financial services industry. Mr. Nagdeman's undergraduate work in economics was at Indiana University, where he was selected to study at Oxford University in that discipline. He completed his graduate work in the honors program at the University of Chicago and was subsequently asked to join their staff. He left academia to go to Wall Street where he held successive positions as director of investment research, director of investment management, and director of marketing for major investment organizations. During that time he also served as a contributing editor for *Barron's* and, over the years, wrote on a diverse range of investment topics. Drawing from his front-line experience, Mr. Nagdeman founded Suasion Resources to provide a viable resource for financial service firms in need of focused and disciplined marketing approaches that achieve revenue growth.

For more than twenty-five years Suasion Resources has created some of the industry's best practices while helping financial services organizations develop effective marketing approaches that

- focus their marketing resources on those initiatives where they will receive the greatest returns

- cost-effectively exploit underutilized areas of marketing
- build brands not simply by promotion but rather by the experience and value that they offer.

This book shares many of the lessons the author has learned concerning concepts and approaches that are often overlooked by financial services marketers.

Notes